What's Biology all about?

Hazel Maskell

Illustrated by Adam Larkum

Designed by Tom Lalonde,
Brenda Cole and Steve Wood

Biology consultants: James Williams,
Dr. John Rostron and Dr. Margaret Rostron

Edited by Rosie Dickins and Jane Chisholm
American editor: Carrie Armstrong

Series advisor: Tony Payton

Contents

Part 4: Where did life come from?

Part 5: Life on Earth

More about biology

Internet links

You can find out lots more about biology on the internet. You can use a virtual microscope to look at cells, watch baby chicks hatch and flowers bloom, zoom into the DNA of a human hand and ask a biologist a question. For links to these websites, and many more, go to **www.usborne-quicklinks.com** and type in the keywords "what is biology".

Please follow the internet safety guidelines displayed on the Usborne Quicklinks Website.
The links are regularly reviewed and updated, but Usborne Publishing cannot be responsible for any website other than its own.

What's biology all about?

Biology is all about life — what it is, how it works and why it is the way it is. It covers all forms of life, from the largest living plants and animals to tiny life forms that are much too small to see; and it's also about where these life forms came from, how they've changed over time, and how they exist side-by-side all over the Earth today.

Here are some of the big questions that keep biologists busy...

What is life?

It's normally pretty easy to tell if something is alive, especially if you can see it without a microscope. But biologists study far weirder, tinier things, which may act as if they're alive in some ways but not in others. Even experts often disagree over whether these things are alive or not.

From big to small

Living things come in all sizes. The smallest are so tiny that you can't see them without a microscope, but the biggest are gigantic — such as blue whales, which can be as long as 16 men lying head to toe.

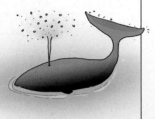

Of all living things, one of the very biggest is a huge fungus in North America. All you can see of it is scattered patches of mushrooms, but below the ground it stretches for miles.

A pitcher of sea water can contain tens of thousands of different kinds of life.

This creature, called *Paramecium bursaria*, is shown about a thousand times larger than real life. Without a microscope, you wouldn't be able to see it at all. It usually lives in stagnant ponds.

Even tinier life forms live inside this one — they are the little green circles. In return for shelter, they make food for their 'host'.

How does it work?

There are some processes that all living things do – although they don't all do them in the same ways. Biologists look deep inside living things to learn how they work – right down to the tiny strands of chemicals that make them what they are.

This is a strand of a chemical called DNA (deoxyribonucleic acid). It contains the instructions that make living things what they are.

Where did it come from?

Some biologists study the remains of ancient living things – some over 3,500 million years old – to piece together a history of life. No one knows how the very first living things formed, but biologists are trying to find out.

Where can you find it?

Living things are found in most places on Earth. Hot, wet places are packed with millions of life forms, and even the coldest or driest areas are almost always home to some. But if life exists on any other planets, we don't know about it.

What are people?
We might like to think we're special, but to a biologist we're just another kind of animal. Specifically, we're a type of ape.

Antarctica is one of the coldest places on Earth, but Emperor penguins can survive and raise their chicks there.

What do biologists do?

Biology is such a huge subject that most biologists specialize in just one area. Here are some of the different kinds of biologists...

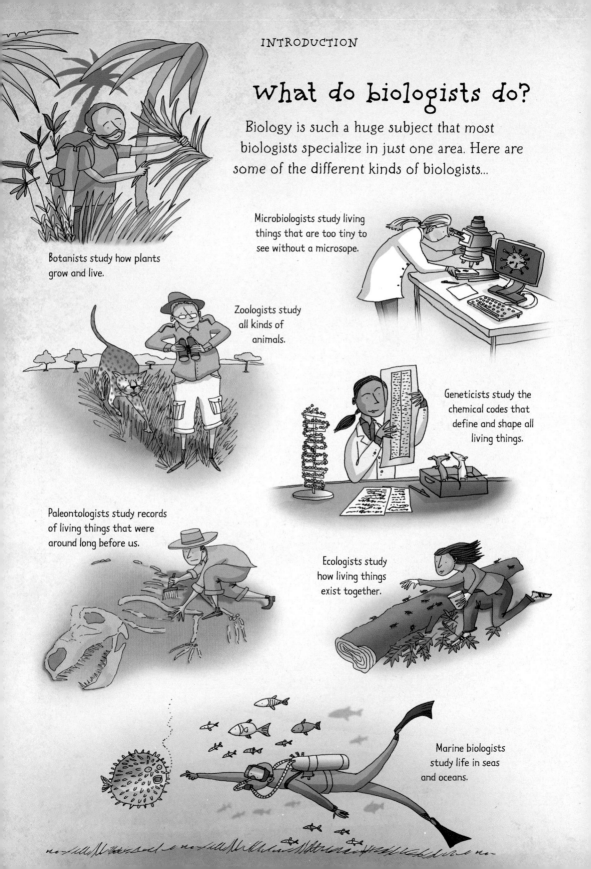

Botanists study how plants grow and live.

Microbiologists study living things that are too tiny to see without a microsope.

Zoologists study all kinds of animals.

Geneticists study the chemical codes that define and shape all living things.

Paleontologists study records of living things that were around long before us.

Ecologists study how living things exist together.

Marine biologists study life in seas and oceans.

What's biology ever done for us?

People have been studying living things for centuries – even if they haven't always called it 'biology'. Their discoveries have made our lives safer, longer and healthier. Here are a few examples...

Hospitals are much safer since experiments showed that keeping things clean prevents germs from causing infections.

Biologists have developed medicines and vaccinations that help to beat diseases. Their studies of the human body have made complex operations possible too.

Louis Pasteur (1822–1895) was a great French scientist who developed the first vaccinations for anthrax and rabies. He also found a way of heating food and drink to kill the germs in them – called 'pasteurization' after him.

Food can be stored safely for longer because scientists discovered germs, and came up with ways to keep food germ-free.

Drinking water became much safer once scientists understood how to rid it of harmful germs.

Joseph Lister (1827–1912) was a Scottish doctor who realized that wound infections were caused by germs. He made hospitals much safer by developing germ-killing antiseptics.

Discoveries of codes, or 'genes', that make us what we are may pave the way for medical breakthroughs in the future.

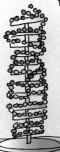

Today, biologists are helping to save animals and plants by studying how they live and what threatens them.

Why are red blood cells shaped like this?

How is this nerve cell like a telephone?

What's this stomach made from?

What do all these tubes do?

Part 1
What's life?

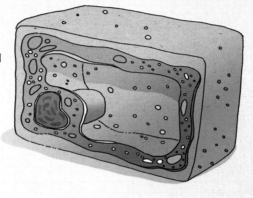

Plant cell

Our planet is teeming with billions of different life forms — from gigantic whales to minuscule microbes. To make sense of it all, the first thing biologists do is define what is and isn't alive. Then they sort living things into categories, to understand the similarities and differences between them. And to see how life works, they look at cells — the basic units that make up nearly all living things.

How can we tell what's alive and what's not?

What links a monkey, a mite and a mushroom? On the surface you wouldn't spot many similarities, if you could even see a mite at all. But they actually have seven things in common with each other, and with every other living thing.

Biologists call these the seven **life processes**...

Moving plants

Put a potted plant on a sunny windowsill. After a few days, look at the direction in which its leaves are facing.

WHAT'S CHANGED?
You should find that the plant's leaves have moved to face the light.

WHY?
Plants need sunlight to make food.

Movement

All living things can move by themselves, even plants – they just move very slowly.

I'm winning!

Nutrition

All living things need food. Animals eat plants or other animals, and plants make their own food using sunlight.

Respiration

All living things release energy from food, in a process called respiration. Most need oxygen to do this.

Waste not...

The most obvious form of excretion might seem to be feces – but actually, feces don't count. They're mainly made up of leftover food that the body can't use, rather than waste chemicals that have been made inside the body.

Excretion

All living things need to get rid of waste chemicals that they have made. They excrete them in sweat or urine, or by breathing out.

10

Reproduction

All living things make new versions of themselves. If they didn't, they would soon die out.

A few plants have very quick reactions. This Venus Flytrap can snap its leaves shut in one tenth of a second.

Sensitivity

All living things can sense what's going on around them. Even though plants don't have eyes or ears, they still react to things such as sunlight.

Artificial life?

Humans have created very lifelike robots. Some can do several, or even most, of the seven life processes. But no one has ever created a robot that can grow or reproduce.

One day you'll be as big as me.

Growth

All living things grow. Some grow to a certain size, then stop. Others continue growing throughout their lives.

So to count something as alive, you must be able to answer 'yes' to all seven categories on this checklist...

Plant

Movement	Yes – slowly
Nutrition	Yes – makes food using sunlight
Respiration	Yes – releases energy in cells
Excretion	Yes – gases and water
Reproduction	Yes
Sensitivity	Yes – to light
Growth	Yes

Truck

Movement	Yes
Nutrition	Yes – it needs fuel to run
Respiration	Sort of – it gets energy from fuel
Excretion	Yes – exhaust fumes
Reproduction	No
Sensitivity	Yes – to the steering wheel
Growth	No

How do biologists divide up living things?

To make living things, or **organisms**, easier to study, biologists separate them into groups, according to what they have in common. This is called **classification**.

There are different systems of classification, but the best-known is called the five-kingdom system, which splits living things into five huge groups, or **kingdoms**.

Animals make up one kingdom, and plants another. The other three kingdoms are fungi, simple tiny organisms called prokaryotes, and more complex tiny organisms called protists.

Smaller sub-groups

Each kingdom is split up into smaller and smaller groups, with more and more in common. The first group is a **division** (for plants) or a **phylum** (for everything else). The next groups are **class**, **order**, **family**, **genus**, and finally **species**. Every kind of living thing has its own species.

Five kingdoms

Animals eat other organisms.

Plants make their own food using sunlight.

Fungi look somewhat like plants, but get food from other organisms.

Protists are very small. Some are like tiny animals, and others are like tiny plants.

Prokaryotes are among the smallest, simplest organisms of all.

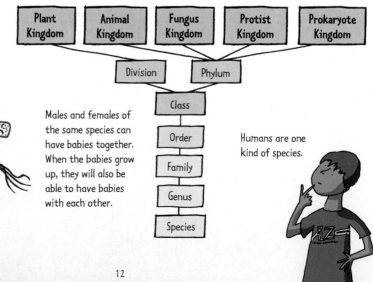

Plant Kingdom	Animal Kingdom	Fungus Kingdom	Protist Kingdom	Prokaryote Kingdom

Division   Phylum

Class

Order

Family

Genus

Species

Males and females of the same species can have babies together. When the babies grow up, they will also be able to have babies with each other.

Humans are one kind of species.

12

What's in a name?

Species have different names in different countries. So to avoid confusion, biologists have one scientific name for each species.

Here is an example of how a single species can be separated out from the whole Animal Kingdom...

Linnaeus' great idea

An 18th-century Swedish biologist named Carl Linnaeus developed the modern classification system, which gives all organisms a two-part scientific name in Latin. He classified thousands of plants and animals himself.

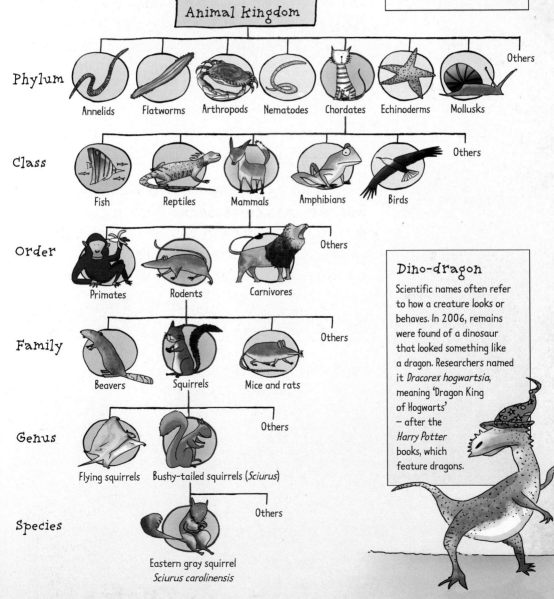

Animal Kingdom

Phylum — Annelids, Flatworms, Arthropods, Nematodes, Chordates, Echinoderms, Mollusks, Others

Class — Fish, Reptiles, Mammals, Amphibians, Birds, Others

Order — Primates, Rodents, Carnivores, Others

Family — Beavers, Squirrels, Mice and rats, Others

Genus — Flying squirrels, Bushy-tailed squirrels (*Sciurus*), Others

Species — Eastern gray squirrel *Sciurus carolinensis*, Others

Dino-dragon

Scientific names often refer to how a creature looks or behaves. In 2006, remains were found of a dinosaur that looked something like a dragon. Researchers named it *Dracorex hogwartsia*, meaning 'Dragon King of Hogwarts' – after the *Harry Potter* books, which feature dragons.

What's this?

Splitting organisms into groups may seem easy, but it's nearly impossible to get a group with no exceptions!

One animal that doesn't quite fit is the platypus. It's a mammal, but it also has a duck-like bill and lays eggs.

The Animal Kingdom

The Animal Kingdom isn't just made up of animals like dogs and dolphins that are easy to recognize. It also includes some you might not think of as animals at all, such as corals and sponges.

What they all have in common is that they get their food from eating other organisms, rather than making their own food, like plants. Animals are also made up of lots of cells, instead of just one.

Animals with backbones

Most of the biggest, heaviest animals are **vertebrates**. This means they have a backbone (made up of bones called vertebrae) to support their bodies. But, although they're the easiest animals to spot, they only make up 3% of the Animal Kingdom.

There are eight classes of vertebrates (of which four are kinds of fish), and they are all grouped into one phylum, called **chordates**. Some are warm-blooded, which means they can control their body temperature. Others are cold-blooded, meaning they can't control their body temperature, and get warmth from the Sun.

Birds are vertebrates with wings and feathers. They lay eggs with hard shells, and are warm-blooded.

Mammals are warm-blooded, hairy vertebrates that give birth to babies rather than laying eggs. Mothers produce milk for their babies to drink.

Reptiles are cold-blooded vertebrates with scales. They live on land and usually lay leathery eggs.

Fish are water-dwelling vertebrates, with scaly skin and gills for breathing. They lay small eggs, and are cold-blooded.

Amphibians are vertebrates that can live on land, but lay their eggs in water. They are cold-blooded.

Spineless creatures

The other 97% of animal species are cold-blooded creatures without backbones, called **invertebrates**. Many have soft, squishy bodies, often surrounded by hard shells. Invertebrates are usually much smaller than vertebrates, although there are some very big invertebrates in the sea, such as squids with tentacles much longer than the tallest person.

Each group of invertebrates has its own phylum. Here are just a few...

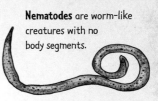

Nematodes are worm-like creatures with no body segments.

Annelids are worm-like and have body segments.

Arthropods have segmented bodies, jointed legs and hard shells. They make up 80% of all animal species, including insects, centipedes, millipedes, spiders, scorpions and crabs.

Mollusks have soft bodies and include snails, octopuses and squid.

Flatworms have flat bodies with no segments.

Echinoderms live in seas, and have tough bodies. They include starfish.

Water-dwelling **cnidarians** have sack-like bodies. They include jellyfish and corals.

Sponges have very simple bodies, which don't even have brains or muscles. They live on the sea floor and hardly move at all.

Rotifers are among the tiniest animals in the world. Most can only be seen with a microscope.

Are spiders insects?

You might think that spiders are insects, but they aren't! Insects and spiders are both arthropods, but they are in different classes.

Insects all have six legs and make up their own class. Spiders belong to a class with eight legs, called **arachnids**, along with ticks, mites and scorpions.

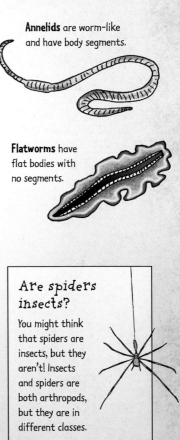

Red Giant

The tallest living thing is a redwood tree in California that's more than 115m (379ft) high – over 63 times higher than a man. This tree is named 'Hyperion', after a giant from Greek mythology.

Thieves

Plants can break the rules too. Dodder is a brownish plant that has hardly any chlorophyll. Instead of making its own food, it winds itself around other plants and steals theirs.

Dodder

The Plant Kingdom

Life on Earth relies on plants, because they make their own food – which can then be eaten by other living things. They make sugars using sunlight, water and a gas in the air called carbon dioxide. To make food, they also need a substance inside them called **chlorophyll**, which is what gives them their green color.

Almost all plants contain tubes for moving food and water around. Most also reproduce by making seeds, which usually contain a tiny baby plant and some food for it, surrounded by a protective case.

Seedy plants

Seed-bearing plants can be divided into two groups: **angiosperms** and **gymnosperms**.

Most plants are **angiosperms** – which means they grow flowers, and their seeds develop in fruits. All angiosperms are in the same plant division.

Grasses

Apple tree

Foxglove

Gymnosperms don't grow flowers, and their seeds often form in cones. Here are the four gymnosperm divisions...

Conifers (including pine and fir trees)

Ginkgoes (of which only one species is found today)

Cycads (including palm trees)

Gnetophytes (certain woody plants)

which plants don't make seeds?

Some plants reproduce using **spores**, which are simpler than seeds. Here are some examples of spore-bearing plants.

Bryophytes are very simple plants that mostly live in damp, shady areas. They are split into three divisions – liverworts, mosses and hornworts.

Ferns and horsetails are the most complex plants that reproduce using spores. They are all in the same division, called *Pteridophyta*.

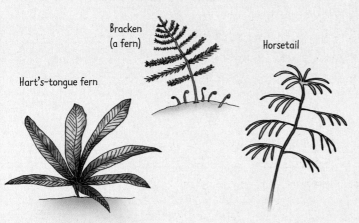

Hart's-tongue fern

Bracken (a fern)

Horsetail

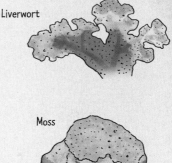

Liverwort

Moss

what about the other kingdoms?

The other three kingdoms in the five-kingdom system contain organisms that can be much harder to spot.

Fungi grow underground or in damp, dark places. Most are made up of masses of tiny threads that feed on dead matter or living organisms. Fungi include mushrooms, molds and single-celled yeasts.

Protists and prokaryotes are so tiny that you can't see them. They are all around, on your skin, in water and the air, and on everything you touch. Prokaryotes are very small, simple organisms. Protists are larger and more complex, and act somewhat like tiny animals or plants. Some even join together to form colonies, such as seaweed.

Just the tip

Toadstools are just a small part of a kind of large underground fungus. The fungus sends up toadstools to release spores above the ground, where they are scattered by the wind.

What are living things made from?

Life comes in an astounding range of shapes and sizes, but nearly all living things are made up of tiny living units called **cells**. Some organisms are only made up of one cell, and others are made of millions upon millions of them.

In organisms with many cells, different cells do different things – from carrying food to creating seeds or babies. Each cell has a particular shape to help it do its job as well as possible. But, although cells can look very different, most contain the same basic structures.

What's in an animal cell?

Here you can see the structures that are found in most animal cells.

The cell in this picture has been enlarged several hundred times. Cells are usually so small that you can't see them at all.

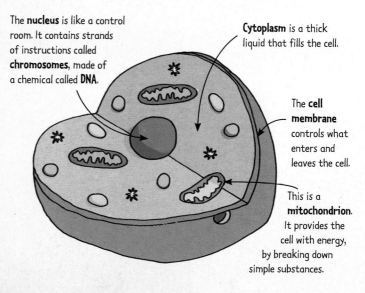

The **nucleus** is like a control room. It contains strands of instructions called **chromosomes**, made of a chemical called **DNA**.

Cytoplasm is a thick liquid that fills the cell.

The **cell membrane** controls what enters and leaves the cell.

This is a **mitochondrion**. It provides the cell with energy, by breaking down simple substances.

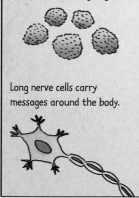

What about a plant cell?

Plant cells usually have all the structures found in an animal cell, and a few extra ones too.

This diagram shows a cell that comes from the top of a leaf.

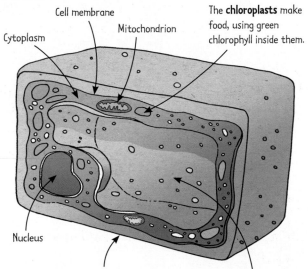

Cell membrane

Cytoplasm

Mitochondrion

The **chloroplasts** make food, using green chlorophyll inside them.

Nucleus

The **cell wall** is a thick layer surrounding the cell, which gives it a fixed shape.

The **vacuole** is a sap-filled cavity that takes up most of the cell.

This photograph shows magnified plant cells, taken from a leaf. The green dots inside the cells are chloroplasts.

Can I see cells?

You can look at some bigger cells using a home microscope. This experiment shows how to look at onion cells.

1. Cut an onion in half, then in half again. Separate the layers.

2. Snap one layer in half.

3. Peel off a thin sheet of onion 'skin'.

4. Put it on a slide, add a drop of water and cover it.

5. Fasten the slide under the clips. Turn the lenses so the smallest one is in position.

6. Use the knobs to lower the lens, then look through

the eyepiece to focus the image. You should see rows of cells.

If you can't see the cells, try a longer lens — but be careful not to bump the slide!

How do your cells stick together?

How do these...

... make up this?

Cells are really small, but they band together to make big, complex organisms, such as humans. And, even though they have different jobs and shapes, joining up is the same step-by-step process for them all.

Cells

Cells group together with other cells of the same type.

This photograph was taken with a powerful microscope, and has been artificially colored. It shows fat cells joined together to make a tissue that stores energy and keeps the body warm.

These **muscle cells** are long and stretchy.

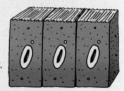

These cells are called **epithelial cells**.

Tissues

Together the cells make something called a tissue. There are many different tissues, including **muscle tissue**, and **epithelial tissue** which lines much of the body's insides.

Most epithelial tissue is thin and delicate.

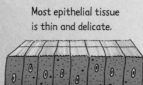

Muscle tissue can contract (bunch up), creating movement.

Organs

Different tissues group together to make **organs**. An organ is a structure – such as the **stomach**, **heart** or **intestine** – which does a particular job in the body.

This is a picture of a stomach. Part of it has been cut away, to show the layers of tissue inside.

This is a cutaway of a tube called the intestine, which transports food and water through the body. It too is made of layers of tissues.

Systems

Organs group together to make **systems**. Humans have 10 systems, including the **digestive system**.

Esophagus

Small intestine

Stomach

Large intestine

The digestive system deals with breaking down food and getting rid of the leftovers.

Organisms

Different systems combine to make an **organism**, which can carry out all seven life processes. (See pages 10-11 for a reminder of what these are.)

A human is one kind of organism.

Splitting cells

If a single cell divides into two, and each divides again, then there'll be four cells. Then if these four divide, there'll be eight. How many divisions would it take to reach 1,024 cells?

The answer is at the bottom of the page.

Why are they called cells?

Cells were discovered in the 17th century, by a scientist named Robert Hooke. Hooke used early microscopes to see that cork was made of tiny chambers. He called them 'cells', after the small, bare rooms where monks lived.

Where do cells come from?

New cells are made when an existing cell splits into two. One cell can divide many times, to make thousands of 'daughter' cells. Plants and animals need all these new cells either to grow bigger, or to replace old or damaged cells.

How do they divide?

Animal cells mostly divide through a process called **mitosis**, in which a series of splits ends with two cells. Each has a full set of instructions inside its nucleus.

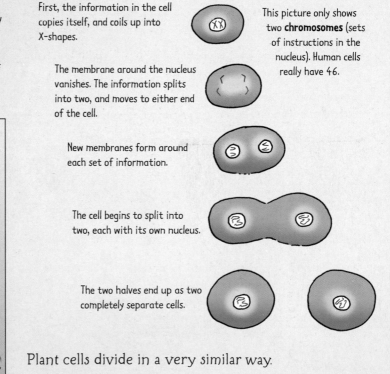

First, the information in the cell copies itself, and coils up into X-shapes.

This picture only shows two **chromosomes** (sets of instructions in the nucleus). Human cells really have 46.

The membrane around the nucleus vanishes. The information splits into two, and moves to either end of the cell.

New membranes form around each set of information.

The cell begins to split into two, each with its own nucleus.

The two halves end up as two completely separate cells.

Plant cells divide in a very similar way.

Answer: from the first division, it'll take 10 sets of division to reach 1,024 cells.

22

What about the very first cell?

Every plant and animal starts off life as just one single cell, which contains the instructions for everything the organism will ever be. This cell divides again and again, starting a chain of cell divisions that can create something millions and millions of times its size.

Most new animals and plants are formed from two special 'half-cells' called **gametes** – one from the mother, and one from the father. Gametes form through a special process of cell division called **meiosis**, which produces cells with only half the usual information.

When gametes come together, the two halves fuse to make a new, complete cell, called a **zygote**. This starter cell contains the instructions to build a brand new organism which will combine features from both its parents.

This is a model of an elephant fetus. Mammals, including elephants, grow from a starter cell into a fully formed baby inside their mother's body.

STEM CELL SCIENCE

Most adult cells can only make copies of themselves – they can't change what *kind* of cell they make. But some cells are different…

Special 'stem' cells can turn into many other kinds of cells. Scientists think stem cells could be used to treat some illnesses and to grow replacements for damaged organs. In 2007, scientists found a way to turn normal adult cells into stem cells. This was a giant break-through, which could lead to many medical advances.

The smallest living things

Plants and animals contain many different cells that work together. But some of the smallest living things are made up of just one cell, and others are so simple that they don't even count as a cell. **Viruses**, the very smallest organisms, are so basic that scientists are still arguing over whether they're really alive at all.

Most single-celled organisms and all viruses are so tiny that they can only be seen with a microscope. They are called 'microorganisms' or **microbes**. Some microbes cause diseases, and are often called germs.

Viruses

Of all the organisms in the world, viruses are the simplest and strangest. They can't carry out the seven life processes alone. Instead, they get into the cells of another organism, or **host**, and use the systems there. So viruses are only alive when they're inside a host. When they are by themselves, scientists say they aren't really alive at all, but 'dormant' (or 'sleeping'). A virus is nothing more than a strand of DNA, or a similar chemical called RNA, surrounded by a protective coat. When it invades a host cell, the DNA or RNA hijacks the cell and forces it to make copies of the virus. When the host cell is full of copies, it bursts. The new viruses are released, and will infect the next cells they come into contact with.

Measuring microbes

Microbes are often measured in 'micrometers', which are thousandths of a millimeter.

Protists are usually between dozens and hundreds of micrometers wide.

Most bacteria measure just a few micrometers.

Viruses are even smaller. They are measured in 'nanometers', or thousandths of a micrometer. Millions of viruses could fit on the dot at the end of this sentence.

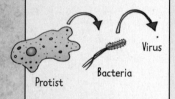

Protist   Bacteria   Virus

This is a photograph of highly magnified influenza viruses. The viruses have been colored artificially.

Bacteria

Bacteria are prokaryotes – very basic cells that lack many of the usual cell structures. They don't even have a nucleus. Instead, their DNA (which is tightly coiled up) floats freely in their cytoplasm. But they are much more complex than viruses, and are definitely alive.

Bacteria are vital for our survival, as they break down dead organisms so chemicals in them can be reused by other living things. Bacteria are useful in other ways, too – for example, some bacteria live inside our bodies and help us to digest food.

Some bacteria have long tail-like strands called flagella, which they beat to move around.

Protists

Protists have complex cells, rather like plant or animal cells. Most are made of just one cell, but others join together to form colonies. There are several different kinds of protists...

Protozoa are single cells similar to animal cells. They eat by engulfing smaller organisms, such as bacteria.

Algae are mostly single plant-like cells. Most have chloroplasts, so they can make food from sunlight.

Some algae join into big groups to form seaweed. These look like plants, but the cells are all similar and don't have specialized jobs.

Hungry protozoa

Protozoa eat bacteria and other protists. To reach its prey, this protozoan pushes part of itself forward and pulls the rest after.

It surrounds the prey with part of its body.

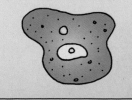

The prey is swallowed up, broken down and absorbed.

Dangerous microbes...

Most microbes are harmless, but some cause diseases. The most deadly, such as the virus that causes HIV, can kill tens of millions of people. Here are some more examples...

Some **bacteria** attack individual cells inside the body, or produce harmful waste products called toxins. They can cause sore throats, food poisoning, meningitis, pneumonia and a deadly disease called cholera which spreads through food and water.

This photograph, taken with a very powerful microscope, shows viruses attacking a bacterium called *Escherichia coli* (or *E. coli*). Some viruses are attached to the cell's surface. Others have already injected themselves into the cell.

Protists can cause diseases such as amoebic dysentery, caused by protozoa attacking the intestine's lining, and malaria, in which protozoa injected through mosquito bites invade the liver and red blood cells.

Overall, however, most bacteria and protists are harmless or even helpful. But **viruses** are only ever destructive, causing illnesses from colds to rabies. The worst kinds can kill millions – the Spanish flu of 1918-19 caused more deaths than the First World War. There are so many strains of each virus that it's impossible to become resistant to them all.

...and how we beat them

Humans have been fighting off dangerous microbes for as long as we've been around, and we're very good at it. Our defenses include nose hairs and tough skins to block germs, stomach acid to kill them in food, and tears to wash them from our eyes.

If these defenses fail, then germ-busting **white blood cells** swing into action. There are two main kinds of white blood cells: **phagocytes** (which engulf germs), and **lymphocytes** (which make structures called **antibodies** that disable germs).

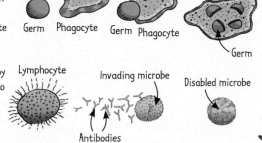

Phagocytes break down germs, and also sweep up any poisonous waste that they make.

Germ   Phagocyte   Germ   Phagocyte

Phagocyte

Germ

The antibodies made by lymphocytes latch onto microbes. Each kind of antibody fights a particular germ.

Lymphocyte   Invading microbe   Disabled microbe

Antibodies

Once your body learns to make an antibody, it remembers how to make it, so if the same kind of microbe attacks again, your body quickly produces the antibodies to fight it off. This means you won't catch the same disease again; you'll have become **immune** to it.

Heat can help to slow down invading germs too, and also helps some white blood cells to do their job. That's why your body temperature often rises when you're fighting off an illness.

But even though our bodies are pros at fighting disease, sometimes they need outside help. That's where medicine comes in...

Avoiding germs

Here are some ways you can avoid picking up or passing on germs...

Many germs travel in droplets in your breath, so cover your nose and mouth when you sneeze or cough.

Germs also cling to your skin, so washing your hands helps to avoid spreading them.

Germs can lurk in raw food. You can kill them by cooking food properly.

New germs can grow on cooked food, but low temperatures slow them down. So it's best to keep food in the refrigerator.

Marvelous medicines

Here are some of the scientists whose brilliant breakthroughs saved millions of lives...

EDWARD JENNER AND VACCINATION

DEADLY SMALLPOX USED TO BE ONE OF THE MOST FEARED OF ALL DISEASES.

PEOPLE KNEW THAT IF THEY SURVIVED SMALLPOX, THEY WOULDN'T CATCH IT AGAIN. IN ANCIENT CHINA, PEOPLE INHALED OLD SMALLPOX SCABS, TO TRY TO CATCH A MILD VERSION. BUT THIS WAS VERY RISKY.

BUT MILKMAIDS HARDLY EVER CAUGHT IT.

AN 18TH CENTURY DOCTOR, EDWARD JENNER, NOTICED THEY OFTEN CAUGHT MILDER COWPOX INSTEAD.

Does cowpox make them immune to smallpox?

JENNER DECIDED TO TEST THIS THEORY WITH A RISKY EXPERIMENT.

FIRST HE INJECTED A BOY WITH COWPOX...

...WHICH DIDN'T MAKE HIM TOO SICK.

THEN HE INJECTED THE BOY WITH SMALLPOX.

If he dies, I'll be tried for murder.

LUCKILY, THE BOY DIDN'T GET SICK.

It works!

NEWS OF THE DISCOVERY SPREAD, AND HUGE NUMBERS OF LIVES WERE SAVED.

WHY DID IT WORK?

SCIENTISTS NOW KNOW THAT COWPOX IS VERY SIMILAR TO SMALLPOX. THE ANTIBODIES THAT FIGHT IT...

...ALSO FIGHT SMALLPOX.

MODERN VACCINES WORK IN THE SAME WAY. A HARMLESS VERSION OF A MICROBE IS INJECTED...

...WHICH TRIGGERS THE PRODUCTION OF CERTAIN ANTIBODIES. THESE WILL FIGHT MORE SERIOUS STRAINS TOO.

THE WORD 'VACCINATION' COMES FROM THE LATIN 'VACCA' - MEANING 'COW'!

28

ALEXANDER FLEMING AND ANTIBIOTICS

ALEXANDER FLEMING WAS A BRILLIANT BIOLOGIST...

...BUT HE COULD BE RATHER MESSY!

ONE DAY HE WAS LOOKING AT SOME OLD EXPERIMENTS WITH BACTERIA, WHEN HE MADE AN ASTOUNDING DISCOVERY.

The mold growing on this dish has killed all the bacteria around it!

HE RESEARCHED THE BACTERIA-KILLING CHEMICAL THAT THE MOLD HAD MADE, AND NAMED IT PENICILLIN.

THEN HE LOOKED FOR A CHEMIST TO TURN IT INTO A MEDICINE.

BUT HE DIDN'T HAVE MUCH LUCK.

A DECADE LATER, TWO SCIENTISTS NAMED HOWARD FLOREY AND BORIS CHAIN USED HIS RESEARCH...

FLOREY

CHAIN

...TO MAKE A VERSION OF PENICILLIN THAT COULD KILL BACTERIA INSIDE HUMAN BODIES.

THEY HAD CREATED THE FIRST ANTIBIOTIC.

PENICILLIN STOPPED COUNTLESS SOLDIERS FROM DYING OF INFECTED WOUNDS IN THE SECOND WORLD WAR.

AT THE END OF THE WAR, FLEMING, FLOREY AND CHAIN WERE JOINTLY AWARDED THE NOBEL PRIZE FOR THEIR WORK...

...AND ANTIBIOTICS HAVE BEEN SAVING LIVES EVER SINCE.

Part 2
How do human bodies work?

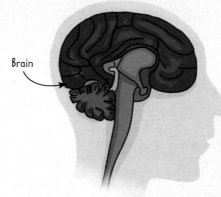

Brain

The human body is so complicated that it's taken biologists centuries to unlock its mysteries, and they're still making new discoveries. Like all animals, human bodies are made up of systems that control everything from breathing and moving to making babies. Fortunately, these systems are so good at their jobs that most of the time we don't even notice they're there. But one thing makes humans very different from other animals — our tremendously powerful brains. They make us the most intelligent species on Earth.

Shape and movement

The human body gets its shape from its **skeletal system**, or skeleton. Without this bony framework, you would collapse into a heap.

Your skeleton also protects your organs from damage, and helps you to move around.

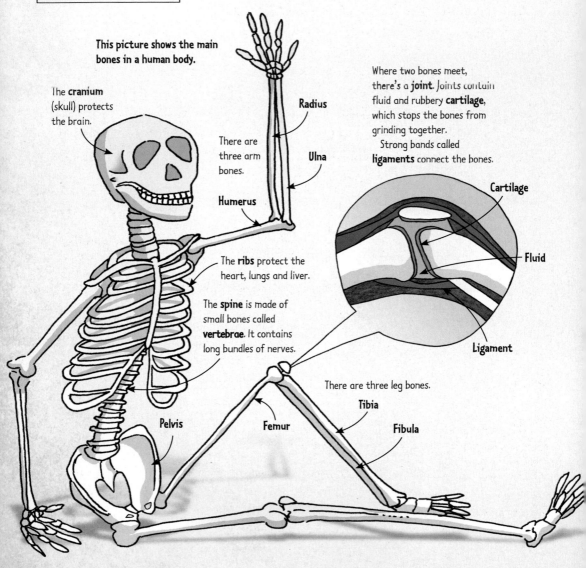

This picture shows the main bones in a human body.

The **cranium** (skull) protects the brain.

Radius

There are three arm bones.

Ulna

Humerus

The **ribs** protect the heart, lungs and liver.

The **spine** is made of small bones called **vertebrae**. It contains long bundles of nerves.

Where two bones meet, there's a **joint**. Joints contain fluid and rubbery **cartilage**, which stops the bones from grinding together.
    Strong bands called **ligaments** connect the bones.

Cartilage

Fluid

Ligament

There are three leg bones.

Tibia

Pelvis

Femur

Fibula

32

How do you move?

Moving seems so simple that it's easy to take for granted. But behind every movement is a complex series of actions, which rely on muscles in your body.

The muscles you use to move around are made up of long, thin cells. Tough cords called **tendons** connect the muscles to the bones on either side of a joint. When you move, the muscle cells get shorter, or **contract**, bunching together to make the whole muscle shorter and fatter. This pulls the bones together.

Muscle cells can only contract – they can't make themselves stretch out to be long and thin again. So muscles usually work in pairs, where only one contracts at a time. As one muscle in the pair contracts, it makes the other stretch. These are called **antagonistic pairs**.

Mighty muscles

Some of our muscles only move when we want them to. Others are out of our control, but these aren't usually attached to bones. Some keep working all the time, such as the heart muscle which pumps dozens of times every minute.

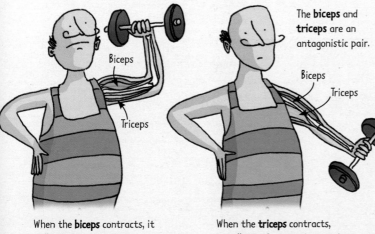

The **biceps** and **triceps** are an antagonistic pair.

Biceps

Biceps

Triceps

Triceps

When the **biceps** contracts, it pulls the forearm up, and the triceps gets long and thin.

When the **triceps** contracts, it pulls the forearm down and straightens out the biceps.

But how does the decision to move get made and communicated to the muscles? It's all thanks to our brilliant brain and hard-working nerves...

Up, down and all around

The joints in your elbow and knee are different from your shoulder and hip joints. Move your body to see if you can figure out how.

You should find that your shoulder and hip joints let you circle your arm and leg, while your elbow and knee only allow your forearm and calf to swing back and forth.

Here's the reason...

Shoulders and hips have **ball and socket joints**. These allow movement up, down and sideways.

Elbows and knees have **hinge joints**. These only let the bone move up or down, not sideways.

Inside the brain

Your **brain** issues commands for all the actions you choose to take, and for many you don't think about, such as controlling your body temperature. A brain is really a gigantic network of thousands of millions of nerve cells, or **neurons**. Each neuron is joined to many others, and new connections are always being made. These connections store your memories, and enable you to think. But it's all so complex that scientists are still finding out how it works.

The **cerebrum** is used for thinking.

The **cerebellum** controls balance and movement.

The **thalamus** receives signals from the body.

The **hypothalamus** keeps the body running smoothly.

The **brain stem** connects to the rest of the body.

All in your head

Sensations such as touch or pain feel as if they're in your body, but really they're all in your head. Nerves in your body send signals to your brain that it interprets as sensations.

Sometimes, a person who has an amputated limb still feels sensations from it. These are made by the brain, which makes them feel as if they come from the missing limb. This is called Phantom Limb Syndrome.

From the brain to the body

Nerves also stretch down your spine and around your body, and whiz electrical signals to and from your brain. When a signal reaches the end of one neuron, a tiny amount of a chemical passes the signal to the next one, until the message reaches its target. Along with your brain, these nerves make up the **nervous system**.

This shows how a neuron works.

Nucleus

1. Branches called **dendrites** receive messages from other neurons.

2. An **axon** carries the signal along.

3. Chemicals pass the signal on to the next neuron's dendrites.

A **myelin sheath** around the axon keeps the signal strong.

Are all neurons the same?

No. There are three main kinds of neurons in your body – all with different jobs.

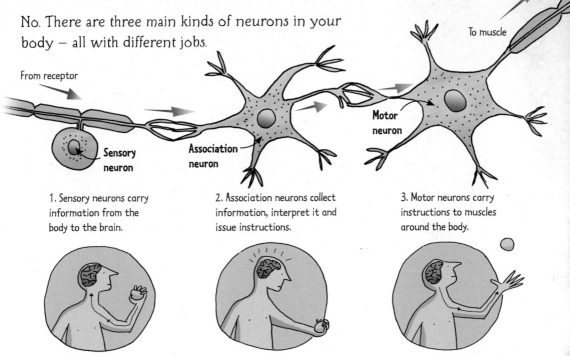

1. Sensory neurons carry information from the body to the brain.

2. Association neurons collect information, interpret it and issue instructions.

3. Motor neurons carry instructions to muscles around the body.

How quickly does it happen?

Messages flash along your nervous system at very high speeds. It only takes a fraction of a second for a signal to travel to your brain and be interpreted, and for an instruction to be issued. There's such a tiny time lag that we don't even notice it.

But in an emergency, even this split second could be crucial. So, to speed things up even more, neurons running down the spine can issue a command for instant action, called a **reflex**.

This is why you react to some things before you've even realized they're happening. Examples include dropping hot objects, or blinking if something gets in your eye.

Mysterious brain

One of the biggest mysteries about the human brain is how it's aware of what it's thinking. This is called **consciousness**. It's what lets us be aware of ourselves, and our actions and decisions. We don't know if any other animals have this ability.

I wonder what she's thinking?

35

Sensing the world

People have five main ways of sensing what's going on in the world around them...

Sight

Light sources send out rays of light. When these rays hit an object, they are altered by it. If they then bounce into your eye, structures called **receptors** send the details recorded in the rays to the brain to interpret.

Lens Retina Optic nerve

To the brain

Pupil

1. Light rays bounce off an object in all directions.

2. Some rays enter an eye through the dark center, or **pupil.**

3. The **lens** focuses the rays on the **retina**, upside-down.

4. **Receptors** in the retina convert the image into signals.

5. The signals travel along the **optic nerve** to the brain.

Hearing

Hearing relies on vibrations, called sound waves, that travel through the air. When these enter the ear, they are processed and sent to the brain.

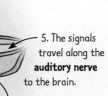

1. The outer part of the ear, called the **pinna**, collects sound waves.

2. Sound waves travel down the **ear canal.**

3. The waves make the **eardrum** and other parts of the ear vibrate.

4. In the **cochlea**, the vibrations are turned into signals.

5. The signals travel along the **auditory nerve** to the brain.

Touch

Your skin contains millions of receptors that respond to sensations such as heat, pressure and pain. The signals they pass to your brain are what creates the sense of touch. Sometimes, the signals make you feel pain, for example if you burn yourself.

Although pain is unpleasant, it's a useful warning that something's wrong. It helps you to react quickly to avoid what's hurting you, and reminds you to protect the damaged part of your body.

Smell and taste

A smell is made up of tiny particles floating in the air. When you breathe in, they touch millions of thread-like receptors deep inside your nose. Different receptors react to different particles, turning the information into signals that whiz off to the brain.

Taste comes from particles in food. The tongue recognizes tastes, although it can only detect five kinds – sweet, salt, sour, bitter and savory.

But, as you eat, particles from the food drift up your nose, adding to the sensation. So the receptors on your tongue and in your nose work together to create taste.

Busy brain

Your brain receives so many different signals that it has to use shortcuts to interpret them. This means it sometimes makes mistakes. For example...

... these gorillas look like they're different sizes, but in fact they're identical. Your brain thinks the top gorilla is farther away – and as things in the distance look smaller, it thinks the top gorilla must be enormous.

Taste test

Try this experiment to see how smell affects your sense of taste.

1. Grate some fruit and vegetables, such as apples and carrots, into separate bowls.

2. Close your eyes, hold your nose and ask a friend to feed you some from each bowl.

3. Can you tell which is which? What about if you do it without holding your nose?

Body fuel

Your body is an incredibly complex machine and, like any machine, it needs fuel to power it. This fuel comes from the food you eat, which gives your body the energy it uses to keep running, as well as chemicals it needs for growth and repair.

The process of breaking down and absorbing food is called **digestion**. The system that deals with it is called the **digestive system**.

What happens when you eat?

Your teeth grind up the food in your mouth, and mix it with chemicals in your spit called **enzymes**. These start to break down the food.

After swallowing, the chunks pass quickly down the **esophagus** into the stomach.

The **stomach** releases enzymes, and acidic juices to kill any germs. Soon the food is churned into a liquid.

The food passes, a little at a time, into the **small intestine**. There, enzymes break it down even further, until the tiny particles can pass through the intestine's lining into the bloodstream.

Leftovers, such as tough parts of fruits and vegetables, pass into the **large intestine** – along with water, dead cells from the intestine, and mucus that has helped move food along. Water is reabsorbed here. Solid waste moves to the **rectum** and passes out of your body as **feces** (or poop).

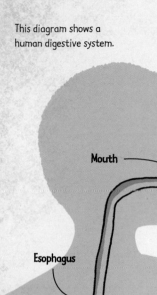

This diagram shows a human digestive system.

Mouth

Esophagus

Stomach

Liver

Large intestine

Rectum

Small intestine

How does your body use food?

Once food particles pass into the bloodstream, they are carried to cells all around the body. Some particles are used to build new cell parts, and others – made of a special sugar called **glucose** – are used for energy.

Some particles are stored in the **liver** for later use, or converted into other useful substances there.

Long tube

The small intestine is small and narrow, but it's really, really long – about four times the length of your whole body.

What kinds of foods are there?

Foods are made of combinations of different types of substances. Here are some of the main groups...

Proteins are chemicals that the body needs for growth, repair and making new cells.

Carbohydrates contain sugars, which provide energy.

People can't digest **fiber**, but its bulk keeps food and water flowing through the intestines.

Minerals and vitamins are chemicals that the body needs. There are many different kinds.

Fats provide energy, keep you warm and are used in building new cells.

Changing tastes

Take a big bite of white bread, and chew it for several minutes. Don't swallow it! Does the taste change?

What happens?

If you keep chewing the bread for long enough, you should find it slowly starts to taste sweeter. That's because it's been broken down into sugars by an enzyme in your spit.

How do you turn food into energy?

To release energy from food, cells need a gas from the air, called **oxygen**. This is so vital that we take over 20,000 breaths of it every day.

How do you get oxygen from air?

Air is only about one fifth oxygen; the rest is made up of other gases, such as nitrogen. But your **respiratory system** can deal with taking in oxygen and getting rid of other gases (especially **carbon dioxide** – see opposite).

When you breathe in, air travels down a pipe at the back of your throat, called the **trachea**. (This is separate from the esophagus, and a flap at the top called the **epiglottis** stops food from entering it.)

Then the air passes along tubes called **bronchi** into big, spongy organs called the **lungs**.

Inside the lungs, the bronchi split into smaller and smaller tubes, which finally end in millions of tiny, moist sacs called **alveoli**.

Oxygen passes through the alveoli's thin walls into the bloodstream. Only about a quarter of the oxygen in each breath is absorbed.

This shows the human respiratory system.

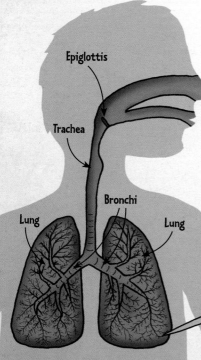

Epiglottis

Trachea

Bronchi

Lung

Lung

The very smallest tubes in the lungs are called **bronchioles**. Each ends in lots of alveoli.

Cluster of alveoli

Blood vessels

Respiration at work

Respiration – or releasing energy from food – is one of the seven life processes. In humans, this happens when glucose from food reacts with oxygen. As energy is released, the glucose and oxygen are turned into water and carbon dioxide (a gas). This can be written as a word equation, like this:

glucose + oxygen → water + carbon dioxide + energy

This reaction takes place in every living cell in your body, as each cell releases its own energy.

See the difference between the air you breathe in and the air you breathe out.

BREATHING IN:
21% oxygen
78.96% nitrogen and other gases
0.04% carbon dioxide

BREATHING OUT:
16% oxygen
78.96% nitrogen and other gases
5.04% carbon dioxide

Feeling the burn

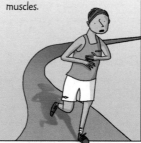

When you exercise, you need more oxygen than normal for respiration. If you don't get enough oxygen, an acid builds up, which causes a burning sensation in your muscles.

Making a noise

Breathing out isn't just useful for getting rid of waste gas. It's also how you talk, sing and shout.

La la laaaaa

Air flowing up your trachea passes folds called vocal cords, making them vibrate. This makes a noise, which you control by relaxing or tightening the cords, and moving your mouth and tongue.

Vocal cords (as seen from above)

Open (low pitch)   Closed (high)

Clearing the waste

Cells need the energy from respiration, but they don't need the carbon dioxide or most of the water. These unwanted leftovers, or **waste products**, are taken away in the blood and used elsewhere or got rid of.

Your body uses water as sweat to keep you cool, or as tears in your eyes. It gets rid of extra water as urine when you use the bathroom. Meanwhile, all the carbon dioxide is carried to your lungs and breathed out.

The blood highway

From the top of your head to the tips of your toes, every cell in your body is connected to your **circulatory system**, which is made up of blood, the tubes which carry it, and your heart. This system acts as a conveyor belt, carrying oxygen, waste and chemicals from food all around your body. It also helps protect you from injury and disease.

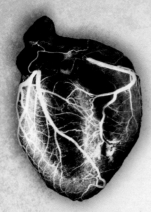

This photograph shows a human heart. The white lines are blood vessels carrying the heart's own supply of oxygen-packed blood.

Changing blood

Blood vessels in your limbs may look bluish green, but it's just an illusion caused by the skin layers. Blood is always red. But blood carrying lots of oxygen is bright red, while blood that's not carrying oxygen is darker.

How does blood get around?

'Circulate' means 'to go around', and that's what blood does in your body. It travels in tubes called **blood vessels**. Some are as wide as your thumb, and others are thinner than a sheet of paper. It takes lots of blood vessels to reach each cell in your body. Laid out end to end, they would stretch several times around the Earth.

This picture shows the contents of a blood vessel, roughly 3,000 times bigger than in real life.

White blood cells fight diseases.

Plasma is a watery liquid. Blood cells and platelets float in it.

Platelets are cell fragments that form blood clots, which keep you from bleeding if you cut yourself.

Red blood cells carry oxygen around the body. You have 25 trillion of these cells, and your body makes 2 million new ones every second. Each lives for about 120 days.

what makes your blood move?

Your blood's journey around your body is controlled by your **heart** – the circulatory system's hard-working pump. The heart is only the size of a fist, but it beats around 100,000 times a day. Each beat squeezes blood-filled chambers inside the heart shut, forcing the blood to race from the heart to the lungs or rest of the body.

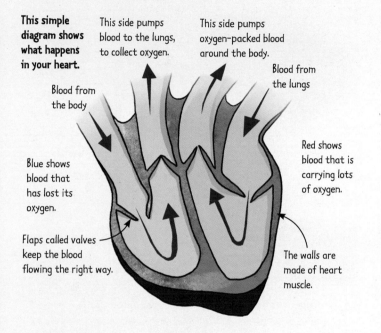

This simple diagram shows what happens in your heart.

This side pumps blood to the lungs, to collect oxygen.

This side pumps oxygen-packed blood around the body.

Blood from the body

Blood from the lungs

Blue shows blood that has lost its oxygen.

Red shows blood that is carrying lots of oxygen.

Flaps called valves keep the blood flowing the right way.

The walls are made of heart muscle.

Counting beats

You can measure the rate at which your heart beats by resting two fingers on the inside of your wrist. Count how many beats you feel in a minute while sitting. Then try counting while doing different things, such as walking or lying down, or after running.

what happens?

You should find your heart rate speeds up when you're more active. This is because your body needs more oxygen, and makes more carbon dioxide to be breathed out.

Your circulation

Arteries (shown in red) and veins (shown in blue) stretch out to all parts of the body. It takes just 45 seconds for blood to travel all around the body and back to the heart.

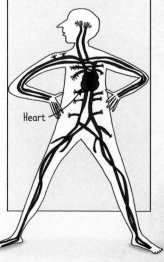

Heart

Vanishing vessels

The vessels leading away from the heart are called **arteries**. They are quite thick, but they split gradually into thinner and thinner tubes. The smallest of these, called **capillaries**, have very thin walls. Food and oxygen pass through these walls into your body's cells.

Cell waste passes through the walls in the other direction. As capillaries fill up with this waste, they form larger tubes called **veins**. These lead back to the heart.

Reproduction

A baby begins when two special cells called **gametes** fuse. This is called **sexual reproduction**. One gamete, called a **sperm**, comes from a man. The other, an **egg**, comes from a woman. Human reproductive systems make gametes and bring them together. A woman's reproductive system also carries the developing baby.

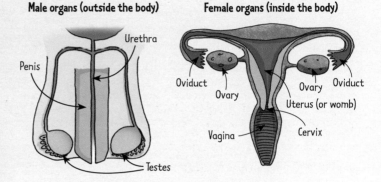

Male organs (outside the body)

Penis

Urethra

Testes

Female organs (inside the body)

Oviduct

Ovary

Vagina

Ovary

Oviduct

Uterus (or womb)

Cervix

Male and female

A male gamete (or sperm) is long and thin. It has a nucleus at the front, and a long tail.

Head

Tail

Nucleus

A female gamete (or egg) is round. It is many times bigger than the head of a sperm.

Nucleus

This is a highly magnified photograph, showing sperm around an egg.

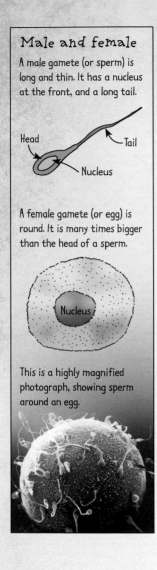

Time of the month

If the egg doesn't fuse with a sperm within a few days, then the extra lining of the uterus breaks down. Blood from it leaks out through the woman's vagina for several days. This is called having a period, or **menstruation.**

Basic baby ingredients

Sperm are made in a man's testes, which hang in a sac outside his body. The slightly cooler temperature there is ideal for sperm production.

A woman is born with lots of eggs already in her ovaries. When she grows up, an egg leaves one of her ovaries about every 28 days, and moves along the oviduct. Meanwhile, her uterus' lining gets extra thick, so it's ready if the egg is **fertilized** (joins with a sperm).

The gametes join through sex. When a man and a woman have sex, the man pushes his penis into the woman's vagina. Muscle movements force millions of sperm out through his urethra into the woman's body. The sperm then swim up to the oviduct. If an egg is there, just one sperm will fuse with it.

Pregnancy and birth

1. The egg and sperm fuse into a single cell, called a **zygote**.

Egg's nucleus

Unsucessful sperm will die.

Successful sperm's nucleus

Oviduct

Embryo

Ovary

To uterus

2. The **zygote** splits again and again to form a ball of cells. Now called an **embryo**, it travels to the uterus.

3. The embryo attaches itself to the lining of the uterus, which provides it with food and oxygen. The cells continue to divide rapidly.

From oviduct

Uterus lining

Embryo

Uterus

Food and oxygen passes from the mother to the baby through a disc-like **placenta**.

The **umbilical cord** joins the embryo and placenta.

Embryo

Uterus

Protective sac

4. After about 2 months, the embryo has a head, arms and legs, and a protective watery sac has formed around it. It is now called a **fetus**.

5. After about 9 months, the baby is ready to be born. The protective sac breaks, and muscle spasms, or contractions, start. These push the baby out of the mother's body, through the cervix and vagina.

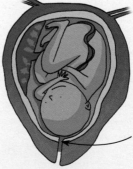

The baby will be pushed out through the cervix, which is here.

45

How do cells know what to do?

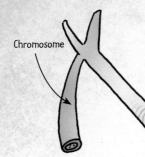

Chromosome

Long strand
of DNA

Gene (individual
instruction)

Each chromosome contains
thousands of genes. Genes are
made of spiral-shaped DNA.

Nearly every one of your cells holds a
complete 'instruction manual' for how your
body works. Different cells refer to different
parts of the manual to do their jobs. Each
manual contains 46 **chromosomes**, which are
strands of coded instructions called **genes**.

DNA (the chemical
that forms genes)

Each manual of 46 chromosomes holds over
200,000 genes, which control how you look, how
your body works, and even how you act. All humans
share similar genes – they're what make us human –
but slight differences mean we're not all the same.

Where did your genes come from?

Children get their genes from their parents. Each sperm
and egg holds a unique set of 23 chromosomes, created
by rearranging a parent's genes, then halving them. If
gametes fuse, these sets join to form a full 'manual'.

As children get their genes from their parents, they
usually look like them. Children also tend to look like
their brothers and sisters, who share very similar genes.

DNA dilemmas

Scientists have just started
to unravel the mysteries of
genes and DNA, and their work
has helped to treat many
terrible illnesses.

But some people worry about
where their research may
lead. For example, should
parents be allowed to choose
their children's genes to
prevent them from inheriting
diseases? How about making
their child smarter or better
looking? And who would be
able to choose – all parents,
or just the richest ones?

46

Pushy genes

Each of the 23 chromosomes that a child gets from one parent is matched by one inherited from the other, to give 23 pairs of mirrored genes. If the genes in a pair contradict each other, only one – called the **dominant** gene – may be used. The other is said to be **recessive**.

For example, the gene for a cleft (or dimpled) chin is dominant over a gene for a smooth chin.

This diagram shows how different genes for cleft or smooth chins can combine.

I have two 'cleft chin' genes.

I have one 'cleft chin' gene and one 'smooth chin' gene.

I have two 'smooth chin' genes.

Here, only the person with two recessive 'smooth chin' genes will have a smooth chin.

But don't write off recessive genes. They may not be used, but they can still be passed on. So two parents with cleft chins can have a child with a smooth chin if they both carry a recessive gene for smooth chins.

This diagram shows how dominant and recessive genes can be passed on in different combinations.

Parents

I have one 'cleft chin' gene and one 'smooth chin' gene.

I have one 'cleft chin' gene and one 'smooth chin' gene.

Children

I have inherited two 'cleft chin' genes.

I have inherited one 'cleft chin' gene and one 'smooth chin' gene.

I have inherited two 'smooth chin' genes.

Genetic genius

The first scientist to make a close study of how characteristics are passed on was an Austrian monk named Gregor Mendel, who lived in the 19th century.

He experimented with breeding pea plants, and noticed patterns in the results. He came up with the idea of dominant and recessive characteristics.

Boy or girl?

Your genes determine whether you're male or female. Women have two 'X' chromosomes, and men have one 'X' and one 'Y' chromosome. The egg always has an X chromosome, and the sperm can have either an X or a Y.

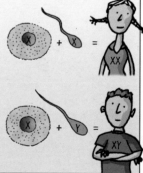

What about other animals?

Other animal species must do the same things that humans do to survive, from eating and breathing to having babies. But they have developed a huge range of strange and startling ways of doing these – as you can see from the examples below.

All animals

For a reminder of the seven life processes common to all living things, turn to page 10. In addition, all animals need to eat to survive.

Skeletons and movement

Animals need to move and support their bodies. Vertebrates have skeletons, but invertebrates (who don't have backbones) keep their shape in other ways.

Fluid fillings

Some invertebrates, such as worms, are packed with fluid. This keeps their bodies firm, and gives the muscles something to push against.

Fluid   Muscle

Hard homes

Many soft-bodied mollusks, such as snails, live inside hard shells. The shell gets bigger as the animal grows.

Shark skeletons

Most vertebrates have bones. But sharks, rays and skates have skeletons made of a tough, lighter material called cartilage – from their spines to their fins.

Outer cases

Arthropods have protective cases, called 'exoskeletons' – 'exo' means 'outside'. Exoskeletons don't stretch, so growing arthropods cast them off to make new, bigger ones.

Boneless bodies

Octopuses don't have skeletons or shells, just very strong, muscular arms and a hard beak for eating. Their lack of bones makes them extra-flexible.

Coral reefs

Coral is made up of tiny animals called polyps. Each has its own miniature exoskeleton, and new polyps build up over the remains of older, dead ones.

Nerves and brains

Almost all animals have nerves that let them move and react to things around them. But some of the simplest animals don't have brains.

Simple jellyfish

Jellyfish have no brains and very simple nerves, which react automatically to what's around them.

Nervy insects

Insects have 'command centers' of large nerve clusters throughout their bodies. Some don't die for a long time even if their heads are cut off.

Clever mollusks

Octopuses, squid and cuttlefish (above) are very smart – they have the most complex brains of any invertebrates.

Loose cells

Sponges are the simplest animals. They don't have a brain or nerves, so their cells act separately from each other.

Senses

Humans mostly use sight to get around. But other creatures rely on different senses – including some senses that we don't have at all.

Super scents

Wolves and dogs have a super-sensitive sense of smell. For every smell receptor that a human has, they have over twenty.

Echolocation

Bats make high clicks, and listen for the echoes to bounce back. From these, they can work out what's around them.

Glowing eyes

Many night animals have a reflective layer at the back of their eyes. As light reflects back out, receptors in the eye have a second chance to pick it up.

Ear

Feeling the way

Many night mammals have touch-sensitive hairs called whiskers. Some can even sense air currents moving around things.

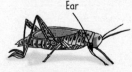

Scattered senses

Many insects have senses in strange places. Crickets hear through their knees, and flies have taste sensors on the ends of their feet.

Electricity

Sharks, such as this hammerhead shark, use nerve cells in their skin to sense tiny electric pulses made by other animals.

Compound eyes

Most insect eyes are made of lots of lenses. These eyes can't see as clearly as ours, but can see over a wider area and detect movements more quickly.

Eating and digesting

All animals need to eat and digest food. But they have different ways of eating it and breaking it down.

Spit soup

Flies cover food with their spit, which breaks it down into a soupy liquid. Then they slurp it up.

Filter feeders

The biggest whales and sharks only eat tiny organisms. They take huge mouthfuls of seawater, then squeeze out the liquid and swallow what's left.

Gobblers

Birds gobble food whole and store it in their crop. Then it moves to their stomach and gizzard to be digested.

Crop

Stomach

Gizzard

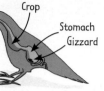

Grazing

Grass is hard to digest, so grazers such as cows and sheep have four sections in their stomachs. Their food is broken down a little more as it passes through each section.

Breathing

All animals, no matter where they live, need oxygen for respiration.

Skin and mouths

Most full-grown frogs and toads can breathe through their skin and the lining of their mouths.

Spiracle

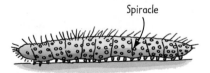

Breathing holes

Insects don't have lungs. Instead, they have holes called spiracles in their exoskeletons, which let in oxygen and release carbon dioxide.

Super lungs

Birds have extra-efficient lungs, which keep fresh and used air separate. This helps the lungs to absorb more oxygen from the fresh air.

Fishy breathing

Oxygen dissolves in water. The water enters fishes' mouths and passes over the gills, which absorb oxygen, similar to underwater lungs.

Hole in the head

Whales and dolphins breathe in and out through holes on their heads. Some whales can hold their breath for up to 90 minutes when they dive.

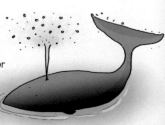

The gills are under this flap.

50

Blood and circulation

Animals must move substances such as oxygen, food and waste around their bodies. Many vertebrates transport these in red blood, but other creatures have different kinds of blood, or even none at all.

Bloodless animals

Some animals, such as flatworms, have such simple bodies that they don't need blood. Instead, nutrients and oxygen pass directly from cell to cell.

Hollow cavity

Arthropods, such as beetles and spiders, have a wide hollow in their bodies. Blood flows through it, carrying food and oxygen to the organs.

The hollow surrounds the organs.

Hearty beasts

Octopuses have three hearts. Two pump blood to the gills, and the third sends it around their bodies.

The hearts are at the back of the head.

Reproduction

Animal reproduction almost always needs a male and female gamete to fuse. But the ways in which it happens varies hugely — as do the ways in which different animal species treat their children.

Fatherless sons

Female Komodo dragons (a kind of lizard) can have male babies without mating, by making gametes that fuse with each other. But they have to mate with a male to have female babies.

Water babies

Most fish release their eggs and sperm into the water, and the gametes join there.

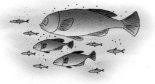

Queen of the hive

Many insects, such as ants, live in huge groups. Just one female, called the queen, lays all the eggs.

Eggs

Baby mammals develop inside their mothers' bodies. But in most other animals, mothers lay eggs and their babies develop inside those.

Eggs laid on land have shells, so the insides stay moist.

Eggs laid in water, such as frogspawn, are usually much smaller and softer.

Stage-by-stage

Frogs, toads and many insects go through three stages as they grow — egg, larva and adult. The larva often looks completely different from the adult.

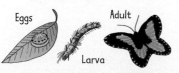

Eggs

Adult

Larva

Beating the odds

Sea turtles lay lots of eggs, then abandon them. Most of the unprotected babies will die, but there are so many that some usually survive.

Part 3
How do plants work?

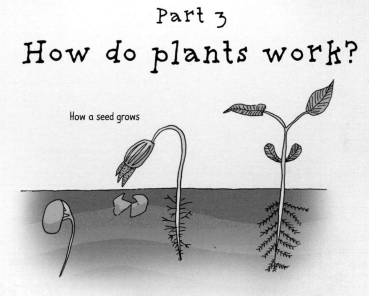

How a seed grows

Plants carpet the Earth, from mosses in the freezing Antarctic wastes to grasses and shrubs in the hottest deserts. In fact, there are so many plants on our planet that from space, much of the land looks green. These plants are vital to our survival, making both the oxygen that we need to breathe and the food we need to eat.

where do plants live?

Warm, damp places such as rainforests are home to over half of all known plant species. There are far fewer kinds of plants around the icy poles, but forests grow even around the Arctic circle, and there are mosses in Antartica. Some tough plants survive high up on mountains, where the air is cold and the soil is thin, or in hot places where it hardly ever rains.

But there are a few plantless places – dark caves, where there is no light to make food, or deep, dark seas and oceans.

Counting plants

Scientists have discovered over a quarter of a million plant species so far – and they are still finding new ones all the time.

Another one!

Ocean 'plants'

Seaweeds look like plants, but really they're much simpler organisms without roots or veins. Instead, each cell takes what it needs straight from the water.

How do plants grow?

Plants grow from sections called **meristems**, where specially adaptable cells divide to make all the different kinds of cells the plant needs. Each plant has lots of meristems, found just behind their root tips and in their stems, especially in their buds.

Many plants grow upward from a meristem at the tip of their stem. But tips may be eaten or damaged, so other plants, including grasses, grow from meristems that lie close to the ground. These plants can grow back quickly after being grazed or mown.

The bud at the stem's tip is called the **terminal bud.** It contains a meristem.

This plant is called St. John's Wort. It grows in all kinds of places, especially grasslands.

Plant parts

This chrysanthemum has a typical plant structure – but not all plants have all of these parts.

Flowers are where gametes are made. These flowers are colorful and scented to help attract insects, which spread gametes between plants.

Leaves collect carbon dioxide and sunlight, which they use to make food.

The **stem** is stiff, and holds the plant upright.

Below ground, the **roots** collect water and nutrients, and anchor the plant firmly in the soil.

What do leaves do?

Plants make food in their leaves. The process is fueled by energy from sunlight, and it's called **photosynthesis** – 'photo' means 'light' and 'synthesis' means 'putting together'.

During photosynthesis, water and carbon dioxide react together to make a sugar called glucose (the food) and oxygen (a waste product). Biologists write this as a word equation, like this:

carbon dioxide + water (+ light energy) → glucose + oxygen

This happens in parts of plant cells called **chloroplasts**.

Plants from dry places, such as this one from an African desert, often store water in their leaves.

What's in a leaf?

Leaves are mostly made up of long **palisade cells** along the top, and round **spongy cells** in the center. Both have chloroplasts, but palisade cells have more. The surfaces of leaves are covered by thin epithelial cells. Water flows from the roots up the stem and into the leaves. If it's not used in photosynthesis, it escapes as water vapor. This is called **transpiration**.

Falling leaves

Deciduous trees lose their leaves before winter. This prevents water loss at a time when ground water may have frozen into ice, which trees can't use.

Evergreen trees don't shed their leaves over winter, as their small, waxy leaves hardly lose any water over the cold months.

This picture shows the structure of a leaf.

The blue holes are **stomata** – pores in a leaf's surface that allow gases and water vapor to flow in and out.

Epithelial cells   Spongy cells

Palisade cells

The little green dots show chloroplasts.

Why do leaves change color?

Leaves are usually green because of **chlorophyll** – a green substance inside the chloroplasts that transfers energy from light into a form the plant can use.

Leaves also contain other substances, which can be red, yellow or orange. Usually the green chlorophyll masks the other colors, but in the fall, the chlorophyll in many trees' leaves breaks down, revealing all the other colors.

Do plants need oxygen?

Just like animals, plants need oxygen to **respire** (release energy from food) and they make carbon dioxide as a waste product. But overall, plants make much more oxygen through photosynthesis than they use up respiring – so there's lots left over for us.

Plants keep respiring all the time, but most only photosynthesize during daylight hours. So at night they only release carbon dioxide, rather than using it up.

Amazing algae

Algae in rivers, lakes, seas and oceans also release oxygen through photosynthesis – though they are protists, not plants. Together, they produce even more oxygen than all of the land plants.

Slow build-up

The amount of oxygen created each year is only small compared to the total amount in the air – but it has been building up over a long time. So the oxygen you breathe today may have been made thousands of years ago.

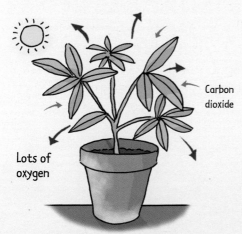

Carbon dioxide

Lots of oxygen

This plant is respiring and photosynthesizing. Overall, it is using up carbon dioxide and producing oxygen.

Oxygen

Carbon dioxide

This plant is just respiring. It is using a small amount of oxygen, and releasing a small amount of carbon dioxide.

Rootless plants

Mosses, hornworts and liverworts don't have real roots, or tubes to transport water and food. Instead they absorb water through their surface, so live in damp places.

Water guzzlers

Some trees absorb more than enough water to fill a bathtub every day.

Meat munchers

Some plants get extra nutrients from animals. For example, insects often fall down the slippery sides of this pitcher plant, and down into a pool of liquid. Then their bodies break down into nutrients that the plant absorbs.

Collecting ingredients

Plants usually absorb water and nutrients through tiny hairs on their roots. These **root hairs** are so small, they slip between tiny particles of soil.

Most root hairs grow near the end of the root. As the root grows longer, old hairs wither and new ones grow farther along. At the tip of the root there's a hard cap, which protects the root as it pushes through the soil.

Root hair

Root cap

Withered root hair

Area that grows

Some plants, such as dandelions, have a thick central root called a tap root. Smaller roots grow out of it.

Other plants, such as grasses, have lots of long, thin roots, all growing out of the stem.

Rooting out a meal

Some plants store food in underground roots, leaves or shoots. Many use it to shoot up quickly in spring. The stores can also provide a tasty meal for animals.

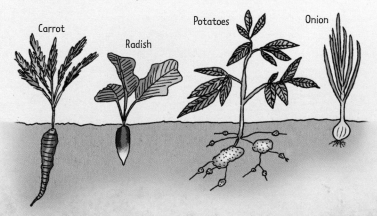

Carrot

Radish

Potatoes

Onion

Transport tubes

Most plants have tissues called the **xylem** and **phloem**, for transporting water and food. Xylem tissue is made of tubes that carry water upward from the roots. Phloem tissue is made of tubes that carry food all around the plant.

Xylem and phloem tissues run through plants in clusters called **vascular bundles**. These support the plant – especially the woody walls of the xylem tubes.

This is a close-up across the middle of a typical plant stem. The colors have been added to show the different parts.

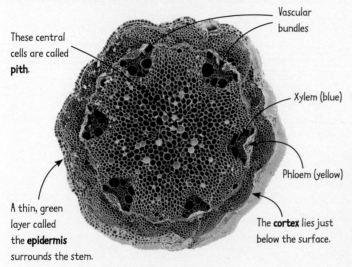

These central cells are called **pith**.

Vascular bundles

Xylem (blue)

Phloem (yellow)

A thin, green layer called the **epidermis** surrounds the stem.

The **cortex** lies just below the surface.

Dying xylem

To see xylem tubes for yourself, try this...

1. Put some water in a container. Add enough food dye to color it.

2. Snap the bottom end off a stick of celery.

3. Put the celery in the water. Leave it for at least an hour.

Look at the end of the celery that's been in the water. You should be able to see where the xylem has taken up the colored water.

Xylem tubes

Why do plants droop?

A healthy plant's cells are packed with watery liquids, making them expand right up to their cell walls and push against each other. This force keeps the plant firm.

But if a plant loses too much water, the cells shrink and stop pushing against each other. So the plant goes limp and wilts. This often happens in summer, when heat dries out the soil.

Tree rings

In trees, xylem and phloem tissue grows in rings. Xylem rings are easy to see, and a new one grows each year.

Xylem rings (one per year)

Phloem rings cluster beneath the bark.

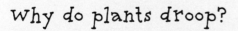

Pollen power

When plants spread their pollen to other flowers, it's called pollination. It can happen in different ways:

Insect pollination

Many flowers make a juice called nectar to attract insects. Pollen clings to the insects, and they carry it to new flowers.

Water pollination

Water plants may use water currents to spread their pollen.

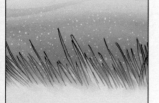

Wind pollination

Some plants have long anthers that scatter pollen as they sway in the wind.

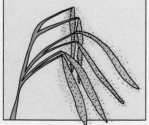

How do plants reproduce?

Most plants use flowers to reproduce. Flowers contain the female gametes, or **ovules**, and the male gametes, or **pollen**. When an ovule and a grain of pollen (often from another flower) join, they form a seed that can grow into a new plant.

What's in a flower?

This picture shows a typical flower structure...

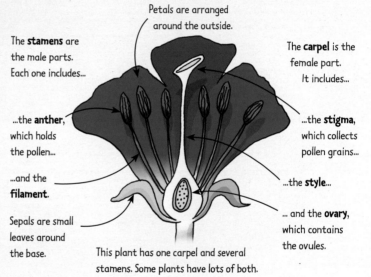

Petals are arranged around the outside.

The **stamens** are the male parts. Each one includes...

The **carpel** is the female part. It includes...

...the **anther**, which holds the pollen...

...the **stigma**, which collects pollen grains...

...and the **filament**.

...the **style**...

Sepals are small leaves around the base.

... and the **ovary**, which contains the ovules.

This plant has one carpel and several stamens. Some plants have lots of both.

How are seeds made?

A seed begins when a pollen grain lands on a stigma. The grain grows a tiny tube through the style to the ovary. Then the grain's nucleus travels down the tube, and merges with the nucleus of an ovule, fertilizing it.

The fertilized ovule divides many times to make a tiny plant embryo. A protective coating surrounds it, forming a seed. Many seeds may form inside an ovary.

From flower to fruit

As seeds develop in the ovary, the petals around the flower wither. The ovary swells and becomes a fruit.

Sowing the seeds

A plant must spread its seeds far and wide, so its own patch of soil isn't overrun. Some plants make fruits that are fluffy or have 'wings' to catch the wind. Others have pods that explode open to scatter their fruits.

Plants also use animals to spread their seeds. Sticky fruits, or fruits with hooks, can catch a ride on passing creatures. Other fruits are eaten by animals, who spit out the seeds or spread them somewhere else in their feces.

How do seeds grow?

If a seed lands in the right spot, with enough light, soil and water, then it **germinates**, or starts to grow.

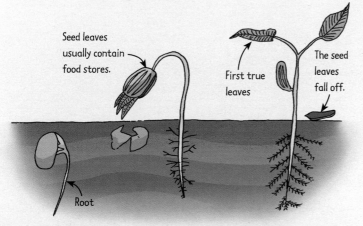

Seed leaves usually contain food stores.

First true leaves

The seed leaves fall off.

Root

When plants first start to grow, they have simple 'seed' leaves. Plants with two seed leaves are called **dicotyledons**, and those with one are **monocotyledons**.

Far and wide

Pea pods dry up, then suddenly split open. The seeds burst out.

Fruits such as this are ideal for hooking onto fur or hairs.

The wind carries these light seeds far away from their parent plant.

Ancient seeds

Some seeds can wait for years to grow into a plant.

In 2005, scientists managed to grow a date palm from a 2,000-year-old seed.

They've named it 'Methuselah' after the oldest person in the Bible.

Simple spores

Liverworts, mosses and ferns don't make seeds. Instead, they reproduce using gametes and **spores** (which are much simpler than seeds). It's a two-part cycle. First, the gametes fuse and grow into structures that make spores; then the spores grow into structures that make gametes. Biologists call this **alternation of generations**.

The brown dots on the underside of these fern leaves are full of spores.

Here you can see how moss plants reproduce...

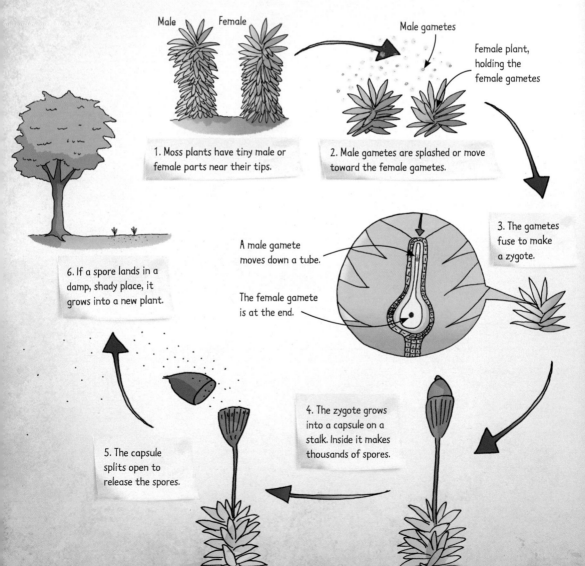

Male   Female

Male gametes

Female plant, holding the female gametes

1. Moss plants have tiny male or female parts near their tips.

2. Male gametes are splashed or move toward the female gametes.

3. The gametes fuse to make a zygote.

A male gamete moves down a tube.

The female gamete is at the end.

6. If a spore lands in a damp, shady place, it grows into a new plant.

4. The zygote grows into a capsule on a stalk. Inside it makes thousands of spores.

5. The capsule splits open to release the spores.

Cloned copies

Many plants can also reproduce by making exact copies of themselves, called **clones**.

Some plants send out long shoots, or **runners**, which put out stems and roots to make new plants. When the new plant is established, the runner withers away.

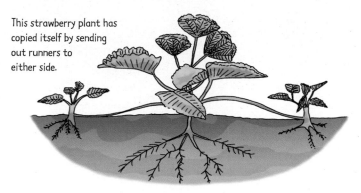

This strawberry plant has copied itself by sending out runners to either side.

Other plants use underground food stores to make copies of themselves. These stores may sprout into new plants, or split to produce two plants rather than one.

Bulbs and sprouts

This onion bulb contains enough stored food to split into two identical plants.

This potato is sprouting into several new plants, which will be identical to their 'parent'.

From bulbs to shoots

Garlic bulbs are food stores that grow into copies of their parent. See how the cloves shoot up into plants...

1. Separate out two cloves from a bulb of garlic.

2. Plant the cloves in a pot full of soil, so that the rounded end is pointing downward.

3. Put the pot somewhere sunny, and water it every day.

4. After about two weeks, you should see new shoots starting to grow from the cloves.

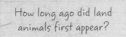

How long ago did land
animals first appear?

What was this and
where did it live?

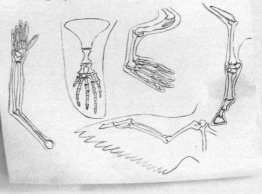

What do humans, whales, frogs,
birds and horses have in common?

Why do these
birds have
different beaks?

How old am I?

Part 4
Where did life come from?

Early amphibian

Over the past few centuries, biologists have
discovered a huge amount about early life,
and how it developed into the organisms we
know today. Their discoveries have challenged
previous ideas of humans' place in the world,
and even today much of their work still
sparks arguments and debates.

How did life begin?

Experts aren't sure exactly how and when life first began. But they have lots of ideas...

Most biologists think the first living things formed in early oceans, which were steaming hot and toxic. They think that chemicals in these oceans reacted together again and again – fueled by sunlight, lightning bursts, volcanic eruptions or hot underwater vents – until they formed molecules that could copy themselves.

Scientists have found traces of living things dating back over 3,500 million years. These ancient organisms were simple water-dwelling bacteria, which trapped particles of mud or sand to form long-lasting stone structures known as **stromatolites**.

Although early microbes such as these were pioneers on a hostile Earth, they had all they needed to thrive – including, eventually, the ability to make their own food by photosynthesis. This produced oxygen, which slowly began to build up in the atmosphere.

What happened next?

Gradually, early microbes developed into more complex life forms. After hundreds of millions of years, some had banded together to make 'multicellular' organisms, in which different cells did specialized jobs. This began a long process of change, which is still going on today.

These stone clumps are made by bacteria. Long ago, structures like these may have been the only signs of life on Earth.

Life in a lab

In 1953, scientists Harold Clayton Urey and Stanley Lloyd Miller set up an experiment to recreate the conditions and chemicals on early Earth. Within just a week, some of the most basic building blocks of life, called amino acids, had formed.

Since then, other experiments have produced more complex building blocks – but never a living organism.

Are we aliens?

Some scientists think the chemicals needed for life were carried to Earth on an asteroid. A few even think that the first living cells arrived like this, after forming elsewhere.

Reading the records

Very few ancient organisms left any record of their existence. But some fragments have survived, and they provide enough evidence for experts to piece together a history of life. The oldest records are stony remains called **fossils**, which can last for many millions of years.

How do fossils form?

1. An organism dies. Its body may decay, but the hard parts remain.

2. The remains are covered by mud, which gets thicker and thicker.

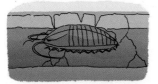

3. The mud hardens into rock. Water and dissolved minerals drip through.

4. Minerals slowly soak into the remains, turning them to stone.

5. The remains are now a fossil. Above, the land slowly changes.

6. Sometimes, the rock wears away or shifts, exposing the fossil.

Sadly, most remains are eaten or rot away before they turn to stone. In particular, those with soft bodies hardly ever become fossils; and remains on land are rarely covered by mud quickly enough. Even when fossils do form, many stay buried deep underground.

Trapped alive

Sometimes animals get caught in sticky situations, such as tar pits or plant sap. As their gooey prison hardens, they are preserved inside.

This termite was trapped in sap 35 million years ago. The sap has hardened into amber.

Trace fossils

Long-dead animals may leave behind other traces, such as tracks, burrows, nests or droppings. These records are called 'trace fossils'.

A large 'sail-backed' reptile left these footprints over 250 million years ago.

From then to now — life's history

This timeline shows how life on Earth developed. Most early creatures were very different from those that are around today.

What happened on land...

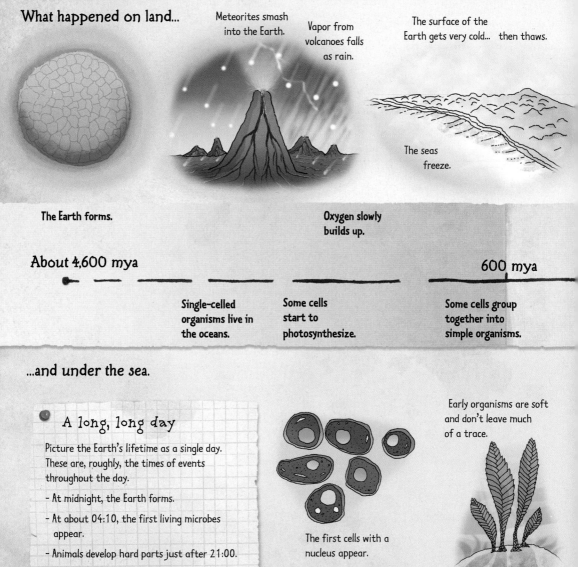

Meteorites smash into the Earth.

Vapor from volcanoes falls as rain.

The surface of the Earth gets very cold... then thaws.

The seas freeze.

The Earth forms.

Oxygen slowly builds up.

About 4,600 mya

600 mya

Single-celled organisms live in the oceans.

Some cells start to photosynthesize.

Some cells group together into simple organisms.

...and under the sea.

A long, long day

Picture the Earth's lifetime as a single day. These are, roughly, the times of events throughout the day.

- At midnight, the Earth forms.

- At about 04:10, the first living microbes appear.

- Animals develop hard parts just after 21:00.

- Dinosaurs first roam the Earth at about 22:45.

- Modern humans appear at around 4 seconds to midnight.

A normal human life span would be over in a thousandth of a second.

The first cells with a nucleus appear.

Early organisms are soft and don't leave much of a trace.

Jellyfish-like animals scrape food from the ocean floor.

68

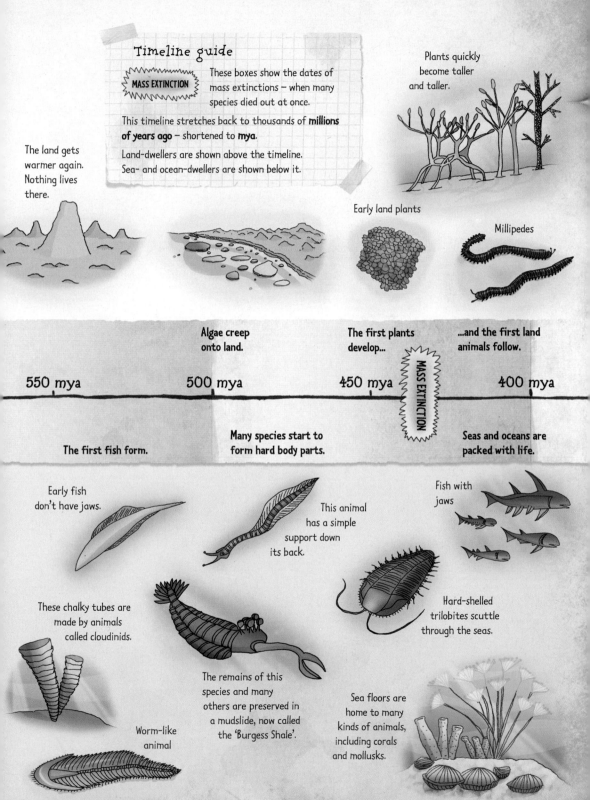

Timeline guide

MASS EXTINCTION These boxes show the dates of mass extinctions – when many species died out at once.

This timeline stretches back to thousands of **millions of years ago** – shortened to **mya**.

Land-dwellers are shown above the timeline. Sea- and ocean-dwellers are shown below it.

Plants quickly become taller and taller.

The land gets warmer again. Nothing lives there.

Early land plants

Millipedes

Algae creep onto land.

The first plants develop...

MASS EXTINCTION

...and the first land animals follow.

550 mya   500 mya   450 mya   400 mya

The first fish form.

Many species start to form hard body parts.

Seas and oceans are packed with life.

Early fish don't have jaws.

This animal has a simple support down its back.

Fish with jaws

These chalky tubes are made by animals called cloudinids.

Hard-shelled trilobites scuttle through the seas.

The remains of this species and many others are preserved in a mudslide, now called the 'Burgess Shale'.

Worm-like animal

Sea floors are home to many kinds of animals, including corals and mollusks.

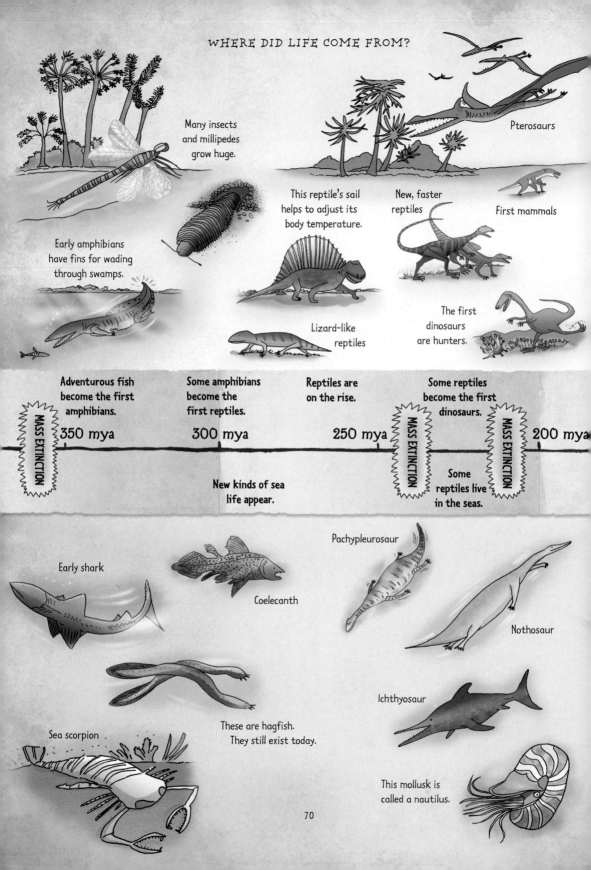

WHERE DID LIFE COME FROM?

Many insects and millipedes grow huge.

Pterosaurs

This reptile's sail helps to adjust its body temperature.

New, faster reptiles

First mammals

Early amphibians have fins for wading through swamps.

Lizard-like reptiles

The first dinosaurs are hunters.

Adventurous fish become the first amphibians.

MASS EXTINCTION

350 mya

Some amphibians become the first reptiles.

300 mya

New kinds of sea life appear.

Reptiles are on the rise.

250 mya

MASS EXTINCTION

Some reptiles become the first dinosaurs.

MASS EXTINCTION

200 mya

Some reptiles live in the seas.

Early shark

Coelecanth

Pachypleurosaur

Nothosaur

These are hagfish. They still exist today.

Ichthyosaur

Sea scorpion

This mollusk is called a nautilus.

70

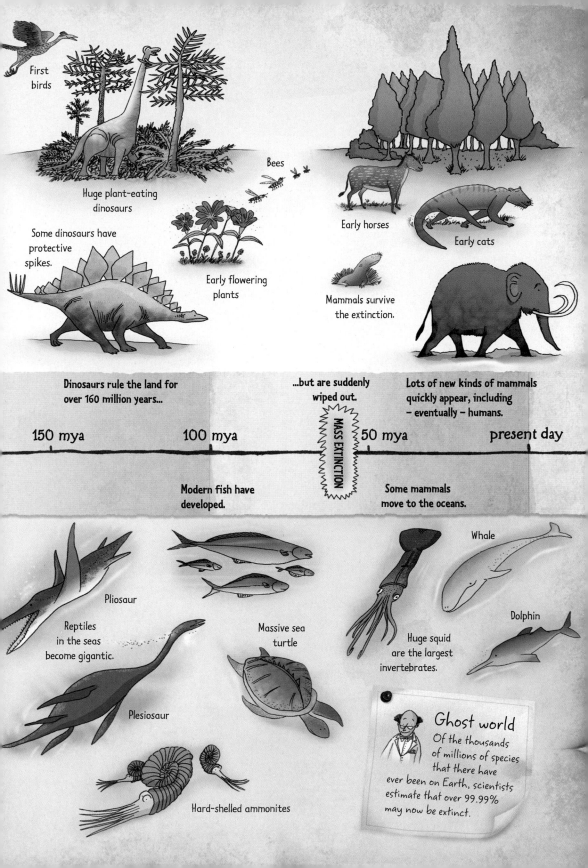

First birds

Huge plant-eating dinosaurs

Bees

Some dinosaurs have protective spikes.

Early flowering plants

Early horses

Early cats

Mammals survive the extinction.

Dinosaurs rule the land for over 160 million years...

...but are suddenly wiped out.

Lots of new kinds of mammals quickly appear, including – eventually – humans.

150 mya   100 mya   MASS EXTINCTION   50 mya   present day

Modern fish have developed.

Some mammals move to the oceans.

Whale

Pliosaur

Reptiles in the seas become gigantic.

Massive sea turtle

Huge squid are the largest invertebrates.

Dolphin

Plesiosaur

Hard-shelled ammonites

Ghost world
Of the thousands of millions of species that there have ever been on Earth, scientists estimate that over 99.99% may now be extinct.

How do new species form?

New species keep appearing — and they don't come out of nowhere. Instead, existing species gradually change and develop into new ones. This is known as **evolution** and it links all living things in a long chain that stretches back to the very first microbes.

Where's the evidence?

A new species will share many features with its ancestors, even if it looks very different. To tell how a species evolved, experts trace these features back through the history recorded by fossils. It's a patchy record, but it shows strands of similarities running through huge numbers of organisms.

More evidence can be found inside organisms alive today. Very different species may have hidden similarities, inherited from a common ancestor. For example, many vertebrates have similar skeletons, suggesting they all evolved from a single species.

Hairy reflex

Goosebumps, the tiny bumps we get on our skin when we're cold or scared, are a reflex inherited from our ancestors.

These bumps appear when muscles raise hairs on our skin. In furry animals, this traps warm air, or makes the animal look bigger. But it's useless in us humans.

These pictures show how different vertebrates share similar sets of bones.

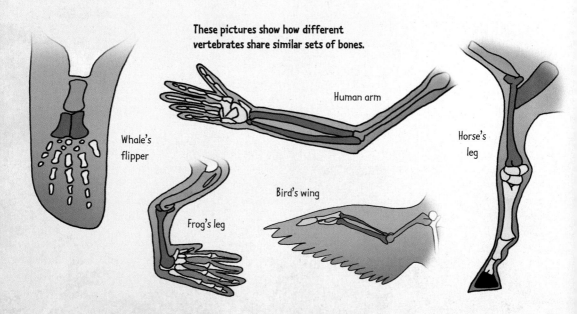

Whale's flipper

Human arm

Horse's leg

Frog's leg

Bird's wing

How does evolution happen?

When a male and female gamete fuse, it almost always produces an individual with a unique set of genes. For example, some gene combinations may result in longer legs or bigger flowers.

Natural resources such as food, water and shelter are always limited, with lots of organisms trying to use them. Species compete with other species to get what they need, and members of the same species compete with each other. Some have genes that make them better suited to where they live. They usually live longer, while others go hungry, get eaten or die out.

The organisms that live longest tend to have the most children. Some inherit their parent's helpful genes, and so have more children of their own. Slowly the helpful genes spread and, after many generations of the best genes being passed along, a new species evolves. This is known as **natural selection.**

Who discovered it?

Charles Darwin (1809-82) and Alfred Russel Wallace (1823-1913) were the first scientists to come up with the theory of evolution by natural selection. In 1859, Darwin published his ideas in a ground-breaking book, called *On the Origin of Species.*

At the time, most people believed all living things had been designed by a creator. They were shocked by Darwin's idea that life's 'design' was really down to competition, inheritance and time.

People are still arguing over evolution today, but it has been consistently supported and built upon by new discoveries, including how genes work.

Growing up tall

Some early grazing mammals ate leaves. Longer-necked ones could eat leaves that others couldn't reach.

The grazers with longer necks had more children, so the gene for long necks spread.

After millions of years, the grazers could reach the treetops. They had become giraffes.

Drifting genes

As well as natural selection, evolution can happen by chance. A gene may change in a way that doesn't give any benefits, but may spread anyway. Or if a disaster wipes out most of a species, the survivors may be lucky rather than well-adapted. This kind of random evolution is known as 'genetic drift'.

How fast does evolution happen?

Evolution is happening all the time, but it's usually very slow. Sometimes species don't change for hundreds of millions of years. But sometimes, evolution suddenly speeds up...

The Earth's landscape is always changing, as immense underground forces push up new islands and mountain ranges. When this happens, species may be split up into separate groups. Each group evolves to suit its new home and, within just a few thousand years, may be on its way to becoming a separate species.

How can extinctions speed it up?

Every so often, huge numbers of species die out at once, in **mass extinctions**. Scientists think there have been at least five of these.

Mass extinctions may happen if the climate changes, if sea levels rise or fall, or if dust from an asteroid collision or volcano blocks out heat and light from the Sun. Species unable to adapt to the new conditions die out, and a wave of new species evolves to fill the gaps.

For example, scientists think the earliest mammals were small mouse-like creatures, and remained so for over 150 million years while dinosaurs ruled the Earth. But the dinosaurs died out in a mass extinction about 65 million years ago, probably when debris from an asteroid collision blocked light and heat from the Sun.

Just a few million years after this, mammals had started to evolve into many new forms, such as cats, horses and monkey-like primates.

Specialized beaks

The Galapagos Islands, west of South America, are home to over a dozen species of finches. They all evolved from the same ancestor, but each has developed a different shaped beak, suitable for getting food on its island.

Ground finches have big, blunt beaks for crushing seeds and nuts.

Tree finches have sharp, thin beaks, for snatching insects up from crevices.

Vegetarian finches have large, strong beaks for nipping fruits, leaves and buds.

Record extinction

The worst mass extinction took place about 250 million years ago. About three quarters of all living species died out, including about 96% of sea-dwellers. Scientists call it the 'Great Dying'. They aren't sure why it happened.

mya stands for 'millions of years ago'. **ya** stands for 'years ago'.

What about humans?

This timeline shows how scientists think humans evolved.

270 mya
Some reptiles develop a sail on their back, which lets them control their body temperature.

200 mya
They evolve into the first, small mammals.

125 mya
Some mammals begin to give birth to their babies.

65 mya
An asteroid hits the Earth, causing mass extinction.

58 mya
The mammals quickly evolve into lots of different species, including tree-dwelling primates.

Mammals survive, probably because they can control their body temperature and don't need much food.

35–25 mya
The first monkeys evolve, followed by the first apes.

7–5 mya
In Africa, some apes begin to walk upright.

2.5 mya
Some develop larger brains, and learn to make tools.

1.5 mya
A species evolves called *Homo erectus*. They learn to hunt and make fires.

200,000 ya
The very first modern humans, *Homo sapiens*, evolve.

10,000 ya
Humans spread around the world. Eventually they start to make towns, farms...

... cities...

Present day

... and books!

Why should meat-eaters care about plants?

HELP!
Why should this shark watch what he eats?

What am I going to have for dinner?

Part 5
Life on Earth

The Earth is home to tens of millions of
species, living everywhere from rainforests to
mountains, cities and the deep blue sea. The
study of where they live, how they've adapted
to fit there and their reliance on their
neighbors is called **ecology**.

Adapting to home

The area where an organism lives is called its **habitat**. Habitats can be any place, from mountaintops to ocean floors, and any size, from a rotting log to a forest. The conditions in a habitat, including temperature, rainfall and soil quality, are described as the **environment**.

Organisms evolve to become well-suited, or **adapted**, to the environment where they live. In fact, many are so well-suited to their environment that they couldn't survive being moved anywhere else.

This habitat has a light, airy, salty and sandy environment.

Awful Arctic?

Temperatures below -30°C (-22°F) and thick snow would finish off most living things. Yet to Arctic organisms, these conditions are perfectly normal...

Polar bears have thick fur and layers of fat to keep out the cold. They're so good at staying warm that they hardly lose any heat at all.

It's hard to walk on the soft snow. Ptarmigans have feathered feet, to spread out their weight and keep them from sinking into snowdrifts.

Some Arctic plants look like cushions – the outer layers protect the insides from winds and cold.

Desperate desert?

Most deserts are bone-dry and blistering hot during the day. But some organisms thrive in this unforgiving habitat...

Camels only need to drink about once a week. Their noses reabsorb most of the vapor in their breath, and they hardly ever sweat.

Many desert animals come out at night, when it's cooler. Jerboas leave their burrows at dusk and may bound over long stretches of sand to find food.

Lots of desert plants spring up during the short rainy seasons. They grow, flower and make seeds in just a few weeks, before the water dries up.

Who does what for whom?

A habitat is usually shared by many species, from microbes and plants to powerful hunters such as lions. All the organisms of a single species in a habitat are called a **population**, and all the populations together are a **community**. An entire community, along with its habitat, is known as an **ecosystem**.

The relationships between different populations are very complex, as each plays a part in keeping the ecosystem running smoothly. Even the biggest, fiercest hunters rely on the plants and microbes around them. So if just one species is removed, the domino effects on all the others can be devastating.

Planet-wide

Ecosystems don't have fixed boundaries – they may be as small as a blade of grass, or as big as an entire country. The biggest ecosystem of all is the planet – where the community is every single animal, plant and microbe.

Here you can see an ecosystem in the African grasslands. Note how each kind of organism relies on all the others.

Grass is food for antelopes.

Leopards eat antelopes. Without hunters such as these, the antelope population would soar and soon run out of grass to eat.

Antelopes' droppings make the soil rich, so grass can grow quickly.

Insects and microbes break down dead matter and droppings. Then what's in them can be reused.

Safe as houses

Sea anemones have stingers on their tentacles, to keep predators away and catch prey. Some small fish have become immune to the stings, and use anemones as safe havens.

Deadly weapons

Although species may depend on each other, the day-to-day lives of individuals tell a very different story. For most, life is a constant battle to avoid being eaten while finding enough to eat. As a result, many species have developed an amazing array of weapons and defenses – from lethal poisons and razor-sharp claws, to hard shells and protective prickles.

Claiming a slot

Each habitat has a limited set of **resources**, such as food, water, space and shelter. The way a species uses these is called its **niche** (a 'niche' means a space or crevice). A species' niche includes where it lives, what it eats and what time of day it comes out.

No two species can share the same niche. If they tried, one would be more successful and drive the other out. The losing species would have to carve out a new niche for itself, or else it would die out.

But species can share the same resources – as long as they don't use them in exactly the same way. For example, giraffes and rhinoceroses spend their days grazing on leaves, but giraffes eat from treetops while rhinoceroses browse on low bushes. And owls and kestrels both hunt for small rodents, but owls do it at night and kestrels do it during the day.

In fact, there are so many ways of using resources that huge numbers of species can live side-by-side – as long as each has its own separate niche.

Different slots

Lions and leopards are very similar animals, and they eat the same food. But they use what's around them in different ways...

Leopards are smaller than lions, and live alone. They climb trees, and hide food up there from lions and other groups of hunters.

Lions live on the ground, in groups. Their large build and teamwork make them the dominant hunters.

Ecosystem meltdown

Species are usually so well-established in their niches that ecosystems are very stable – as long as the conditions remain the same. But any changes – such as disease, climate change or the arrival of a foreign species – can be disastrous. Even if just one species is affected to begin with, the results can soon spread across the whole ecosystem.

Are all species equally important?

Not always, no. Although all species in a community have important roles, a single species may hold the key to it all. This species may do something that affects the habitat, keeps a balance between other species, or provides shelter or food.

For example, elephants are vital to African grasslands, as they clear away trees and stop forests from growing. And in flat North American prairies, ground squirrels build huge burrows that provide shelter for other species.

These species are called **keystone species**, after the top 'keystone' in an archway, which holds the other stones in place. But ecosystems are so complex that it can be hard for biologists to determine which, if any, is a keystone species.

Australian species

Australia is an isolated country with very unusual native animals.

For example, almost all Australian mammals, such as kangaroos and koalas, give birth very early and carry their tiny babies in pouches.

But through the centuries, humans have brought over foreign species such as dingoes (wild dogs) and rabbits. These have taken over most niches, and many native species have now become extinct.

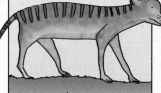

Thylacines like this one were wolf-like hunters that became extinct after dingoes took over their niche.

Sea otters are a keystone species in many coastal areas, where they are the only animals that eat sea urchins.

Without them, sea urchins quickly multiply and destroy the ecosystem.

what's for dinner?

In an ecosystem, energy from food is constantly being passed between organisms. Animals that get their energy from eating other animals are called **carnivores**, and those that get it from plants or algae are called **herbivores**. Humans and all other animals that eat both animals and plants are known as **omnivores**.

Plants and algae are called **producers**, because they produce their own food through photosynthesis. The food they make is vitally important — it's the fuel that powers all the other organisms.

This is an example of a food chain. The arrows point from what's being eaten, to who's doing the eating.

You can show who eats what by making a line of organisms, called a **food chain**. Food chains start with the producer, and lead up to the top carnivore.

Plants   Insects   Meerkats   Eagles

Each ecosystem contains many different food chains, which can be linked together in a **food web**.

This shows a food web for a community living in African scrubland.

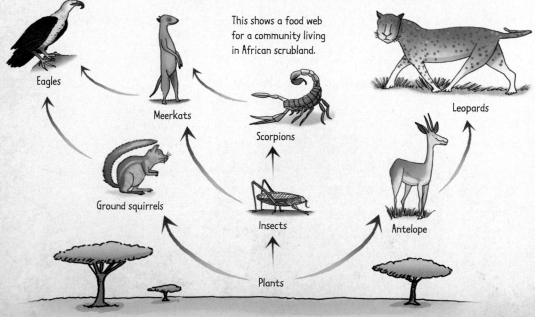

Eagles

Meerkats

Scorpions

Leopards

Ground squirrels

Insects

Antelope

Plants

How many, and how big?

To show the size of the different populations in a food web, biologists sometimes draw a stack of bars called a **pyramid of numbers**. The length of each bar reflects how many of that species there are. Each species eats what's in the bar below it.

Here's an example of a pyramid of numbers:

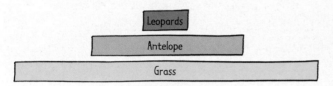

| Leopards |
| Antelope |
| Grass |

Each species needs lots of what it eats, so each bar is shorter than the one below it. And if the producers are small plants such as grass or algae, their bar will be the longest of all.

But, sometimes, the producer may be a big plant such as a tree, which by itself provides food for many animals. Then, the pyramid of numbers looks like this:

Pyramid of numbers

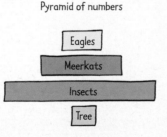

| Eagles |
| Meerkats |
| Insects |
| Tree |

In this case, a pyramid showing the physical size and weight of each population gives a clearer idea of what's going on. This is called a **pyramid of biomass**.

Pyramids of biomass are always widest at the bottom.

Pyramid of biomass

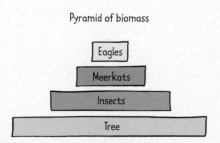

| Eagles |
| Meerkats |
| Insects |
| Tree |

Poisoned chain

Sometimes man-made poison or waste gets into a food chain, like this...

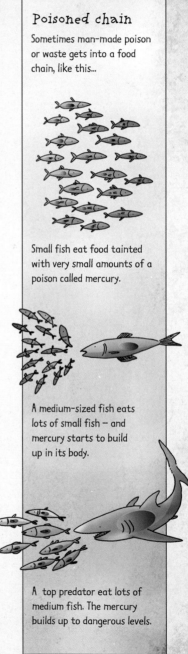

Small fish eat food tainted with very small amounts of a poison called mercury.

A medium-sized fish eats lots of small fish – and mercury starts to build up in its body.

A top predator eat lots of medium fish. The mercury builds up to dangerous levels.

How do humans fit in?

Like all animals, humans compete with other species; but it's no longer a fair fight. For millenia we've altered our habitats to suit us, often threatening the species that live alongside us. Here are just some of the problems we've caused, and some possible solutions.

Habitat destruction

The problem: Habitats such as grasslands and forests are cleared to make space for towns, cities and farms. Some forests are cut down for wood.

The results: Species lose their homes and food sources. With nowhere to live and nothing to eat, many die out.

Plan of action: Huge reserves that no one may build on have been set up, as well as protected 'green belts' around cities. Some farmers leave wild areas free on their land, to give wild animals somewhere to live.

Pollution and waste

The problem: Factories, power plants and cars release harmful chemicals and gases. Farmers and gardeners may also use chemicals to make plants grow better, or to kill pests. We throw away lots of waste.

The results: Chemicals may harm ecosystems, especially in rivers and lakes. Some gases combine with water in the air to make acidic rain, which kills plants and animals. Mountains of waste are building up.

Plan of action: Experts are finding ways to reduce the production of harmful gases. Some farmers no longer use harmful chemicals. Many countries have campaigns to cut waste, and lots can be recycled.

Then and now

For every person who lived a thousand years ago, it's estimated there are more than 22 alive today. The current human population is 6,700 million, and scientists predict it's going to continue growing and growing...

Lifeless lake

Unnaturally high levels of nutrients in this lake have caused huge amounts of algae to grow. When the algae die, bacteria use up oxygen in the water to break them down, suffocating all the fish.

Climate change

The problem: We burn fuels such as coal and oil to get energy to run everything from cars to factories.
The results: Burning these fuels releases gases such as carbon dioxide, which traps heat from the Sun. Most experts agree this affects weather, making the Earth warmer. Many species can't adapt to the new climates.
Plan of action: Some countries have agreed to reduce their carbon dioxide production by using less coal and oil. Less harmful energy sources can be used instead, such as wind, moving water and the Sun.

Polar bears hunt seals on sheets of sea ice that form each winter. But recently the ice has melted more and more quickly. This makes it hard for polar bears to hunt, and many may end up starving or drowning.

Why should I care about biology?

As far as we know, the only life in the entire universe is right here on this planet. Yet because of us, species are disappearing at an alarming rate – making many experts think we're causing the next mass extinction.

The study of biology has helped us to understand life, and now biologists are vital in learning how to protect it. So taking an interest in biology could, quite literally, mean the Earth to future generations.

Safe havens

This family of cheetahs lives on a big nature reserve in Kenya. There, they are protected from poachers and can live and hunt naturally. Without dedicated workers to set up and manage reserves like this, we'd have lost far more species.

More about biology

Now you know what biology's all about,
turn the page to find out more about the
brilliant biologists of the past and
the super scientists of today...

Biology through the ages

People have been studying living things for thousands of years, even though they only began to describe what they were doing as 'biology' about 200 years ago. Here is the story of biology so far, including the most influential biologists and their breakthroughs and achievements.

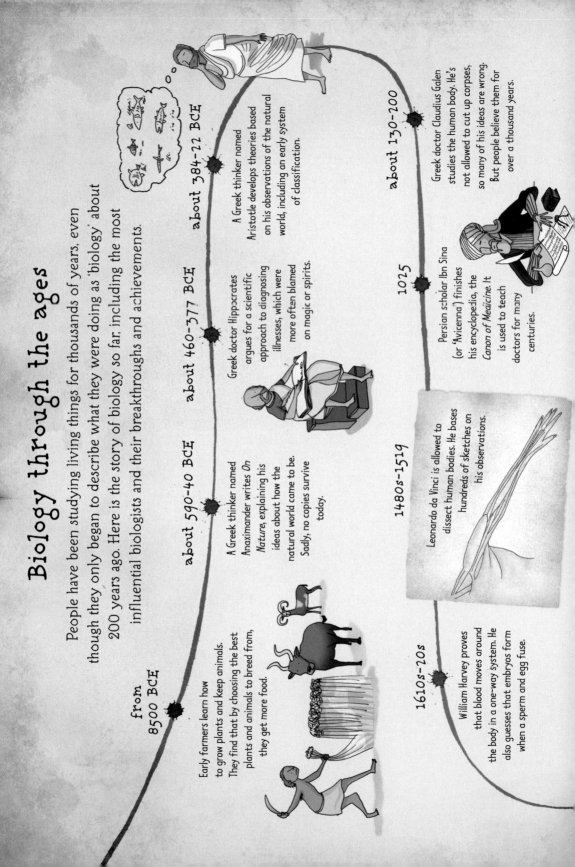

from 8500 BCE

Early farmers learn how to grow plants and keep animals. They find that by choosing the best plants and animals to breed from, they get more food.

about 590-40 BCE

A Greek thinker named Anaximander writes *On Nature*, explaining his ideas about how the natural world came to be. Sadly, no copies survive today.

about 460-377 BCE

Greek doctor Hippocrates argues for a scientific approach to diagnosing illnesses, which were more often blamed on magic or spirits.

about 384-22 BCE

A Greek thinker named Aristotle develops theories based on his observations of the natural world, including an early system of classification.

about 130-200

Greek doctor Claudius Galen studies the human body. He's not allowed to cut up corpses, so many of his ideas are wrong. But people believe them for over a thousand years.

1025

Persian scholar Ibn Sina (or 'Avicenna') finishes his encyclopedia, the *Canon of Medicine*. It is used to teach doctors for many centuries.

1480s-1519

Leonardo da Vinci is allowed to dissect human bodies. He bases hundreds of sketches on his observations.

1610s-20s

William Harvey proves that blood moves around the body in a one-way system. He also guesses that embryos form when a sperm and egg fuse.

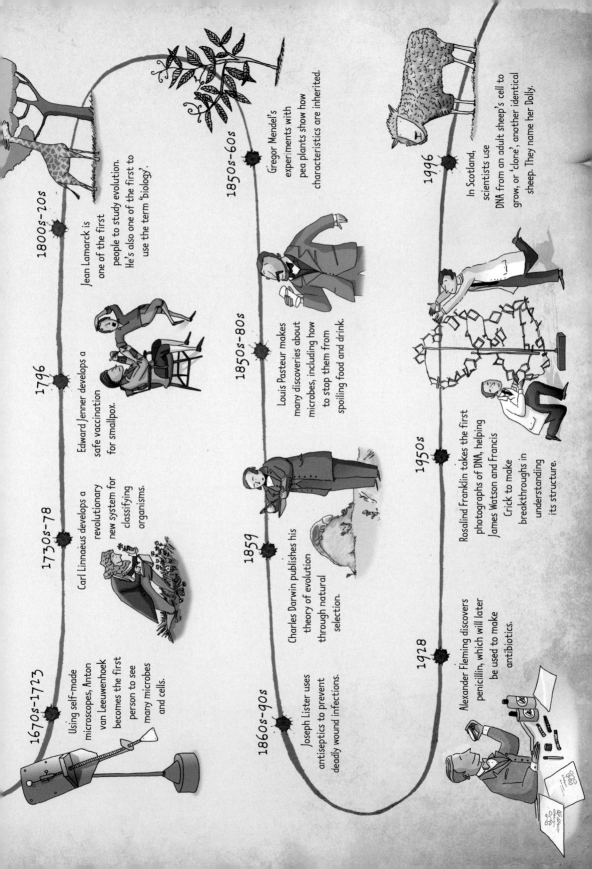

1670s-1723

Using self-made microscopes, Anton van Leeuwenhoek becomes the first person to see many microbes and cells.

1730s-78

Carl Linnaeus develops a revolutionary new system for classifying organisms.

1796

Edward Jenner develops a safe vaccination for smallpox.

1800s-20s

Jean Lamarck is one of the first people to study evolution. He's also one of the first to use the term 'biology'.

1850s-60s

Gregor Mendel's experiments with pea plants show how characteristics are inherited.

1850s-80s

Louis Pasteur makes many discoveries about microbes, including how to stop them from spoiling food and drink.

1859

Charles Darwin publishes his theory of evolution through natural selection.

1860s-90s

Joseph Lister uses antiseptics to prevent deadly wound infections.

1928

Alexander Fleming discovers penicillin, which will later be used to make antibiotics.

1950s

Rosalind Franklin takes the first photographs of DNA, helping James Watson and Francis Crick to make breakthroughs in understanding its structure.

1996

In Scotland, scientists use DNA from an adult sheep's cell to grow, or 'clone', another identical sheep. They name her Dolly.

How does biology work?

What is science?

Science comes from the Latin word *scientia*, meaning 'knowledge'. It's the study of how things work, and is divided into three areas:

Biology is the study of life.

Chemistry is about the substances that make up the world.

Physics is the study of the laws that rule our universe.

Biologists (and all other kinds of scientists too) come up with ideas that explain something about the world. They base those ideas on things they've seen, or that other biologists have written about.

Then they have to see if their ideas are right. To be a real scientist, it isn't enough to say that what you *think* is true, or that you believe it, or that it's common sense. You have to *prove* it's right (or at least, not wrong), by doing experiments that back it up. When an idea can be tested through experiments, it's called a **hypothesis** (unlike the many ideas people have that can't be tested scientifically).

Top scientists write about their experiments in journals, so other scientists around the world can try them too. If other experts agree there is enough evidence, the hypothesis becomes a **theory** — that means, it's the accepted, tested and most likely explanation of why something is the way it is.

How do experiments work?

An experiment must be a fair test of an idea.

1. Hypothesis
This is where you explain what your idea is. It also usually includes predictions of what you expect the results of the experiment to be.

2. Method
This describes how you're going to do the experiment. It includes a control, which is the 'normal' situation; and the experiment, which is like the control but with one key difference. That way, if the results vary, you know it must be because of that one thing.

3. Results
These record the outcome of the experiment (including the control).

4. Conclusion
This is where you interpret the results. Did they support the hypothesis? Have you changed or rejected your hypothesis after seeing the results?

Here's an example of a simple scientific experiment:

1. Hypothesis
'Plants need water to live. Without water, a plant will die.'

2. Method
Take two plants, and label them A and B. Make sure they're the same kind of plant, get the same amount of light and all other conditions are the same. For two weeks, water plant A (the control, or normal situation), but don't water plant B.

3. Results
Plant A is healthy. Plant B has wilted and died.

4. Conclusion
The only difference between the plants was that one was watered, and one wasn't. So plant B probably died because it didn't have any water. This result supports the hypothesis.

However, there might be reasons why this experiment wouldn't work. The control (plant A) might have a disease and die too; or, if it's used to dry conditions, it might die from being over-watered. So, to get reliable results, it's best to try the experiment many times with lots of different plants.

Are scientists ever wrong?

Yes, scientists get things wrong all the time! They may misinterpret experiments, get bad results, or not be able to test ideas until the right technology is invented.

But what every good scientist wants most of all is to discover how things really work — even if that means admitting to mistakes along the way. So if their ideas are proved wrong, they're always prepared to change what they think, and move on.

> 'The one who seeks truth ... submits to argument and demonstration'

This was the philosophy of one of the first scientists to use fair, rigorous experiments.

Ibn al-Haytham, an 11th-century scholar, based his theories about light and vision on his own observations, rather than what people usually assumed was true.

He argued that scholars shouldn't trust anyone's ideas without carefully considering the evidence for themselves.

Glossary

Words in *italics* have their own separate entries.

adaptation When a *species* alters over time to become better-suited to the place where it lives.

algae *Protists* which make their food through *photosynthesis*. Some kinds join to form seaweed.

angiosperm A plant that flowers and produces seeds inside a fruit.

antagonistic pair Two muscles that work alternately to move a body part. As one contracts, the other one relaxes.

antibiotic A medicine used to treat illnesses caused by *bacteria*.

antibodies Chemicals made by some white blood cells, which attack and disable invading germs.

artery A blood *vessel* that carries blood away from the heart.

bacteria Single-celled *organisms* with a simple cell structure and no *nucleus*.

cell The basic unit of life, made of structures floating in cytoplasm and bound by a membrane.

chromosome A long strand of genetic information found in the *nucleus* of a *cell*. Human cells contain 46 chromosomes. Each chromosome is made up of sections called *genes*.

chlorophyll The green substance in *chloroplasts* that absorbs energy from light for *photosynthesis*.

chloroplast The structures inside plant *cells* that contain *chlorophyll*.

classification A way of sorting *organisms* into groups based on shared characteristics.

cloning When an *organism's genes* are copied to make an identical organism. Many organisms use cloning to reproduce.

community All the members of all the different *species* that live together in a *habitat*.

digestion The process by which food is broken down inside the body, to be used as fuel.

DNA (deoxyribonucleic acid) A very long molecule that contains coded instructions for all that happens in a *cell*, and much of the structure and operation of the whole *organism*.

ecosystem A combination of a place and its conditions, and all the *organisms* that live there.

embryo An early stage in the formation of a new *organism*, when it has basic body structures, but before its *systems* are working together properly.

environment The conditions in a *habitat*.

enzymes Chemicals made by *cells* to speed up reactions.

epithelium A *tissue* that lines a cavity inside the body.

evolution When *species* change into new species over time. It mostly happens through *natural selection*, although other processes can play a role too.

extinct A term describing a *species* that has died out.

fertilization When a male and female *gamete* fuse together to make a *zygote*.

fossil The remains or traces of a long-dead *organism*, turned to stone after millions of years spent buried underground.

fruit Part of a plant that grows after *fertilization* of the *ovules*, to surround one or more seeds.

gamete A sex cell, holding half the *genes* of a normal *cell*. A new individual forms when a male and female gamete fuse.

gene Part of a *chromosome* that holds instructions for one or more characteristics. Humans have over 200,000 genes.

glucose A type of sugar used to provide energy. Animals get it from food, and plants make their own.

gymnosperm A plant that produces seeds, but not flowers or *fruits*.

habitat The place where an *organism* lives.

invertebrate An animal without a backbone.

kingdom The first, and largest, subdivision that biologists divide living things into; for example the plant and animal kingdoms.

life process One of the seven basic functions that biologists look at to decide if something is alive or not.

mammal A group of *vertebrates* who have hair, make milk to feed their babies, and most of whom give birth.

mass extinction When huge numbers of species die out over a short time.

meiosis A kind of cell division that results in *gametes* with half a set of *genes*.

meristem Part of a plant made of *cells* that divide to make the plant grow, found in shoots, buds and roots.

microbe A tiny living thing that can only be seen with a microscope. Most are single-celled *organisms*.

mitosis A kind of cell division that results in two *cells*, each with a full set of *genes*.

natural selection The way in which the most successful individuals' *genes* spread through a *species*, gradually causing a new *species* to evolve.

nervous system The *system* made up of the brain and nerves, which relays and reacts to messages.

neuron A nerve *cell*, used to carry messages around the body.

niche A *species'* slot in an *ecosystem*, including how it uses the resources. Each species has its own niche.

nucleus The structure in a *cell* that holds its *chromosomes*.

nutrients Vital substances that *organisms* can't make for themselves, so must obtain from soil or food.

organ A collection of *tissues*, joined together into a structure that does a particular job (such as a heart).

organism Any living individual.

ovule A female *gamete* of a flowering plant, found within the flower.

phloem Tubes that carry food all around a plant.

photosynthesis The process by which plants make their own food from water and carbon dioxide, in a reaction powered by energy from sunlight.

pollen Tiny powdery grains, which are a flowering plant's male *gametes*.

pollination The transfer of pollen to a stimga (often on another flower), to fertilize an *ovule*.

producer Any *organism* that makes its own food rather than eating other organisms.

prokaryote Single-celled *organisms* with simple *cell* structures and no *nucleus*. *Bacteria* are prokaryotes.

protist A single-celled *organism* with a complex *cell* structure and *nucleus*. *Protozoa* and *algae* are protists.

protozoa *Protists* that get their food from digesting other *organisms*.

receptor A nerve ending or *cell* that detects information about the outside world.

reflex An action taken automatically by the nervous *system*, which happens without you thinking about it.

respiration The process that releases energy from food; it usually needs oxygen and makes carbon dioxide.

sexual reproduction A way of reproducing in which a male and female *gamete* fuse, creating a new individual with a unique set of *genes*.

species A group of *organisms* so similar that they can breed together, producing children that can also breed.

sperm A male *gamete* of an animal.

spore A basic reproductive *cell*, made without *fertilization* by the simplest plants.

stomata Holes in a leaf which water and gases pass through.

system A collection of *organs* which together do a particular job in the body, such as *digestion*.

tissue Many *cells* of the same type, grouped together to form part of an *organism*.

transpiration Loss of water from a plant through its leaves. This draws up water from the roots.

vaccinaton Infecting an *organism* with a harmless form of a germ, to make it produce *antibodies* that will safeguard against the germ in the future.

vein A blood *vessel* that carries blood to the heart.

vertebrate An animal with a backbone.

vessel A tube that carries liquid around an *organism*, such as blood or sap.

virus A very simple particle with some characteristics of a living organism.

xylem *Vessels* in a plant that carry water from the roots to the leaves.

zygote The first *cell* of a new *organism*, made when a male and female *gamete* join.

Index

Acknowledgements

Every effort has been made to trace and acknowledge ownership of copyright. If any rights have been omitted, the publishers offer to rectify this in any future editions following notification. The publishers are grateful to the following individuals and organizations for their permission to reproduce material on the following pages: (t=top, b=bottom)

p4 © Visuals Unlimited/Corbis; **p5** Art Wolfe/Science Photo Library (SPL); **p11** GK Hart/Vikki Hart; **p16** © Kevin Schafer/Corbis; **p17** Hans Eggensberger; **p19** John Durham/SPL; **p20** Steve Gschmeissner/SPL; **p21** © Jupiterimages/Brand X/Corbis; **p23** David Barlow Photography/Artem Model; **p24** James Cavallini/SPL; **p26** Lee D. Simon/SPL; **p40** James Stevenson/SPL; **p42** SPL; **p44** D. Phillips/SPL; **p54** Winfried Wisniewski/FLPA; **p55** © Phil Degginger/Alamy; **p56** © Frans Lanting/Corbis; **p58** © Nick Garbutt/naturepl.com; **p59** (t) Steve Gschmeissner/SPL; (b) © Hiromitsu Watanabe/amanaimages/Corbis; **p62** © Phillippe Clement/naturepl.com; **p66** John Reader/SPL; **p67** (t) © Layne Kennedy/Corbis; (b) © Lester V. Bergman/Corbis; **p78** © Sally A. Morgan; Ecoscene/Corbis; **p81** © Norbert Wu/Minden Pictures/FLPA; **p84** © Steven David Miller/naturepl.com; **p85** (t) © Tom Mangelsen/naturepl.com; (b) © Suzi Eszterhas/Minden Pictures/FLPA

Series designer: Stephen Moncrieff
Art director: Mary Cartwright
Additional designs: Samantha Barrett and Anna Gould
Image manipulation: John Russell
Picture research: Ruth King